ALL THINGS
OZ

ALL THINGS OZ

Words by L. FRANK BAUM
Illustrations from THE WILLARD CARROLL COLLECTION

Photographed by RICHARD GLENN

Introduction by WILLARD CARROLL

Edited by LINDA SUNSHINE

Designed by TIMOTHY SHANER

CLARKSON POTTER/PUBLISHERS
NEW YORK

Published by Clarkson Potter/Publishers, New York, New York.
Member of the Crown Publishing Group,
a division of Random House, Inc.
www.randomhouse.com

CLARKSON N. POTTER is a trademark
and POTTER and colophon are registered
trademarks of Random House, Inc.

Printed in Singapore

Library of Congress Cataloging-in-Publication Data
is available upon request.

ISBN 1-4000-4848-6

10 9 8 7 6 5 4 3 2 1

FIRST EDITION

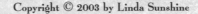

Contents

Introduction by Willard Carroll 10

Foreword by Linda Sunshine 12

LIFE IN A FAIRY COUNTRY

Anything Is Possible 15

Many Queer Things 16

Laws in the Land of Oz 18, 27

Living in Oz and
    the People of Oz 20

Weather, Time, and Land Mass . . . 22

In the Civilized Countries 25

The Reason Most People Are Bad . . 28

The Fairy Amendments 30

I Have Lived Here Many Years 33

A Day in the Life of Glinda 34

The Legal System in Oz 36

Anyone Who's Sorry 39

She Rules Oz 43

We Are Loved for Ourselves Alone . 45

Ruling Class 47

A Grand Title 51

Every Road Leads Somewhere 54

Money 56

Everyone Is Happy 59

If We Walk Far Enough 70

You Have to Ask 75

Don't Slump Down! 86

Read This Tree 90

Dining in Oz 97

Animal Life in Oz 112

A Crowd of Monkeys 114

Pity the Poor Meat People 126

Birds Are the Luckiest
    Creatures of All 129

Contents

Military Life in Oz 132
Favorite Sayings in Oz 140
Booktionary 142
The More You Fish 146
Oz Mermaids 148
The Land of the Munchkins 253
The Wisdom of Oz 282
Earth Is a Beautiful Place! 344

FOUR FRIENDS AND TOTO, TOO!

Dorothy

Girl Power 154
What Should We Do Next? 157
Never Give Up 158
Simplicity and Kindness 177
Like Many Other Girls 179
One Magical Art 180
I Came from Kansas 181
A Once-in-a-While Princess 182

Toto

The Only Dog in Oz 121
Her Little Black Dog 199
Toto's Secret 200
Toto and the Tin Woodman 209

The Cowardly Lion

In Joyous Greeting 217
King of Beasts 222
Why He Isn't a Coward 227

The Tin Woodman

The Tin Woodman Lectures
    on Money in Oz 57
Anyone Can Be Conquered 130

Contents

A Roman Gladiator 139
When We Have the Least Reason . . 163
My Head Is Quite Empty 230
At Home with the Tin Woodman . . 234
We Are Not Built the Same 251
The Last End of a Wait 278

The Scarecrow

The Best Thinker 82
Uncomfortable Feeling 85
Is the Scarecrow Alive, Grasshopper? 125
A Means of Escape 135
In an Emergency 136
Dorothy Meets the Scarecrow 258
Scarecrow Affirmations 262
Near to Quarreling 261
Don't Call Me a Fool 269
All Wrong, Somehow 272
There Are Worse Things 277

THE WITCHES, THE WIZARD AND THE WONDERS OF OZ

Harboring Wicked Creatures 286
The Way with Wicked People 291
Dorothy Was Innocent 292
Kissed by the Witch of the North . 296
The Witch Did Not Bleed 299
Wizard's Words of Wisdom 302
A Very Bad Man 304
What They Wanted from Him . . . 305
A Bag of Magic 306
Any Enchantment 308
Autobiography 309
Never So Wonderful 312

Contents

Confessions of the Wizard of Oz . . . 314

Only a Humbug Wizard 317

Jigsaw Puzzle 330

Love Has Nine Lives 336

MUNCHKIN TALES

That Makes Me Angry! 40

Thirty Heads Are Better Than One 48

The Wisdom of the Shaggy Man . . . 80

The Lunch-Box Tree 92

A Kansas Dog 204

At Home with the Scarecrow 274

Blinkie 288

Her Pretty Shoes 294

Love at First Sight 334

LITTLE WIZARD STORIES

The Cowardly Lion and
the Hungry Tiger 101

Little Dorothy and Toto 185

The Scarecrow and
the Tin Woodman . . . 239

ADVENTURES IN OZ STORIES

The Emerald City: A Visitor's Guide 61

A Wogglebug Education 77

A Visit to Utensil Town 165

What Toto Lost 211

The Cowardly Lion Gets
the Evil Eye 219

The Fuddles Fall Apart 321

POEMS AND SONGS

Sweet, Fresh, Golden Straw 88

The Woggle Bug Song 118

Song of the Fishes 122

Johnny Dooit 208

Contents

And When She Tired 226

Oz Never Did 233

T Is the Tin 237

The Hollow Men 249

Safe in the Funny Little
    Munchkins Town 255

The Scarecrow's Lament 266

S Is for Scarecrow 271

Higgledy, Piggledy, Dee 333

TV Theme Song 339

OTHER VOICES, OUTSIDE OF OZ

Kindergarten Magazine,
    October 1900 52

Michael Patrick Hearn ... 68, 301, 340

Actual Listing 72

Mark Teague 73

Bruce Degen 116

Robert A. Heinlein 145

L. Frank Baum 151, 252, 346

Aljean Harmetz 160

James Thurber 107

Gita Dorothy Morena 202, 231

The Baum Bugle, February 1966 ... 224

C. Warren Hollister 228

Harry Neal Baum 276

Elizabeth Gilbert 281

Ruth Plumly Thompson 284

Joey Green 318

Ray Bolger 342

Further Reading 346

International Wizard of Oz Club .. 347

About the Art 348

Acknowledgments 352

SHARED JOY

by Willard Carroll

More than one hundred years after its initial publication, *The Wonderful Wizard of Oz* continues to exert a pleasurably overwhelming influence upon our individual and collective experience, both conscious and—the true test of a seductive phenomenon—subconscious.

Countless editions of the book continue to be published worldwide; the MGM movie still garners big ratings when aired on networks or cable; stage productions abound; and it's estimated that every 3.2 seconds someone, somewhere in the world, utters the phrase: "Toto, I've a feeling we're not in Kansas anymore."

Okay, I made up that last part. But you get the idea.

And it is, after all, the *idea* of Oz that engages us. The marvelously, confidently eccentric inhabitants of the Land of Oz—a utopian society that was conceived, nurtured, and explored in the boundlessly imaginative mind of L. Frank Baum—touch us with their struggles, their triumphs, and their embracing of all things and people unique.

Anyone self-deluded enough to describe themselves as "normal" need not apply for a visa.

Oz is more than just a place. Baum's creation of an alternate world goes beyond mere geographical fantasy. It showcases an alternate

worldview—one distinguished by compassion, tolerance, quests for identity, peace and a heck-of-a-lot of serious fun.

I like to think Oz isn't a place to escape to; it's a place to take with us on our individual journeys and travails. And, let's face it, the company—be it a Scarecrow, a Tin Man, or a chicken named Billina—can't be bettered.

Oz has now bridged several generations. Many of us first saw the movie as children with our families—time shared which takes on more than just a nostalgic hue, but which, in essence, established for many the very definition of "shared experience." And, it's an experience we look forward—even crave—to share with another generation . . . and another and another.

That's a fairly terrific way to propagate that not-so-elusive-after-all sense of genuine community that is at the heart of Oz. Oz can be, should be, *is* a shared experience, perpetually evolving into shared joy.

For Oz is all things joyful, the idea endless, and the possibilities continuously surprising. Oz is without boundaries.

Sure, it may all be wrapped up in a fantasy, but it's a magnificent one.

I think I'll go there now.

EDITOR'S NOTES by Linda Sunshine

I began this project with Willard Carroll by reading the fourteen novels about the Land of Oz that L. Frank Baum wrote, starting with *The Wizard of Oz* in 1900. (After Baum's death in 1919, more than thirty Oz books were penned by other writers but I decided to concentrate solely on the work of the original creator.) In almost every book, I discovered wonderful words of wisdom, endearing philosophical ideas, cheery optimism and Baum's obvious love of the English language in puns, jokes and rhymes. Many made me laugh out loud.

I asked Willard if Baum had ever published any short stories and he handed me a rare copy of a 1913 edition of *Little Wizard Stories of Oz*. I was completely captivated by this collection, and three of the six stories in this hard-to-find volume are reprinted here in their full glory, along with their original illustrations by John R. Neill, as "Little Wizard Stories."

In each of the novels, I found long passages describing strange and wondrous Oz adventures that I thought could stand alone as short stories. These include tales about an army of spoons that took Dorothy and Toto as prisoners, a big bug who taught college, and a very puzzling group of folks called the Fuddles. I've presented these delightful accounts as "Adventures in Oz Stories" and illustrated them with art from many diverse sources.

I also discovered shorter passages (some only a paragraph or two) that are perfect examples of Baum's utterly original imagination; these appear as short, short stories called "Munchkin Tales." Many times I was stopped dead in my reading by a single sentence or a line of dialogue of such profound charm and wisdom that I wanted to offer it as a one-line quote—a sort of Oz affirmation.

Willard directed me to other sources that featured original poems and song lyrics by Baum and I've included several of them here, too. Finally, I added quotes from an

eclectic group of writers including James Thurber, Robert A. Heinlein, Aljean Harmetz, and Michael Patrick Hearn. For all of these excerpts—long and short—I've provided the title of the books from which they came, in the hopes they will inspire readers to delve into the original novels.

All of the art is, of course, from The Willard Carroll Collection. Some pieces date back to 1900; some come from far-away lands and many have never before appeared in print in this country. My editor, Annetta Hanna, was especially interested in the origins of the art, so I've added resource notes for all the images at the end of the book.

"In the Land of Oz much wisdom and many things may be learned," Baum wrote in *The Tin Woodman of Oz* (1918). So what did I learn from reading Baum? Well, in the Land of Oz, good always conquers evil and there is only one absolute rule to obey: Behave Yourself. If I had to describe the Baum philosophy in two sentences, it would be these: Be kind, be brave and keep moving forward. Everything will turn out all right in the end. Now that was not a bad philosophy for the early 1900s and, to my mind, is just as relevant at the dawn of the twenty-first century.

L. Frank Baum wrote thousands and thousands of pages about Oz and I've condensed his work down to a mere 352. If he took you on a leisurely stroll through Oz and I can only offer a whirlwind tour, well, never mind; once there, you're sure to find joy. "Everyone in the Emerald City is happy," Baum tells us, "they can't help it." So be happy, have a safe journey, watch out for those winged monkeys, and for goodness' sake, behave yourself.

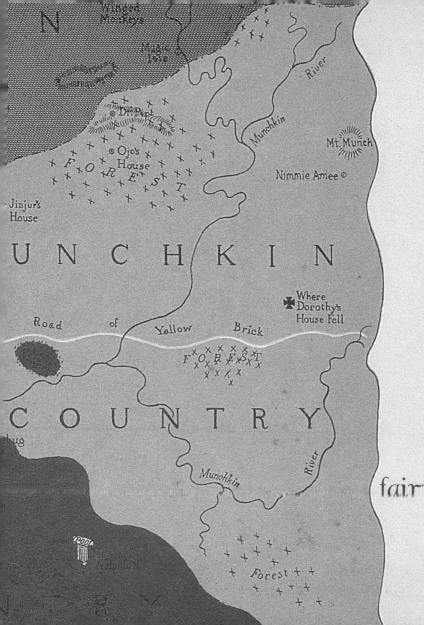

In the
Land Oz,
anything
is possible.
For it is a
wonderful
fairy country.

—OZMA OF OZ, 1907

You're likely to see many queer things in the Land of Oz, sir. But a fairy country is extremely interesting when you get used to being surprised.

—**The Wizard**, *THE EMERALD CITY OF OZ*, 1910

Laws in the Land of Oz

The people of Oz have but one law to
obey, which is: "Behave Yourself."

—*THE TIN WOODMAN OF OZ*, 1918

No one in Oz has the right to destroy
any living creature, however evil they may
be, or hurt them or make them unhappy.

—*THE EMERALD CITY OF OZ*, 1910

It's against the law to pick
a six-leaved clover in Oz.

—*THE PATCHWORK GIRL OF OZ*, 1913

Living in Oz

If you can prove to the Princess Ozma that you are honest and true and worthy of friendship, you may indeed live in Oz all your days, and be as happy as everyone there.

—THE ROAD TO OZ, 1909

The People

In the Land of Oz, people have not changed in appearance since the fairies made it a fairyland. Since no one grows old or dies in Oz, it is difficult to say how many years anyone has lived.

—GLINDA OF OZ, 1920

Weather
The weather
is always
beautiful in Oz.

—*THE EMERALD CITY
OF OZ, 1910*

Land Mass

The Land of Oz is a pretty big place, when you get to all the edges of it.

—*THE LOST PRINCESS OF OZ*, 1917

Time

Time doesn't make much difference in the Land of Oz.

—*GLINDA OF OZ*, 1920

In the civilized countries I believe there are no witches left; nor wizards, nor sorceresses, nor magicians. But you see, the Land of Oz has never been civilized, for we are cut off from all the rest of the world. Therefore we still have witches and wizards amongst us.

—**Glinda**, *THE WONDERFUL WIZARD OF OZ*, 1900

Laws in the Land of Oz

No persons in the Land of Oz are permitted
to work magic except Glinda the Good
and the little Wizard who lives with
Ozma in the Emerald City.

—*The Tin Woodman of Oz*, 1918

The penalty for chopping leaves from
the royal palm-tree is to be killed seven
times and afterward imprisoned for life.

—*The Marvelous Land of Oz*, 1904

Laws were never meant to be understood
and it is foolish to make the attempt.

—*The Marvelous Land of Oz*, 1904

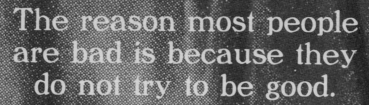

The reason most people
are bad is because they
do not try to be good.

—THE EMERALD CITY OF OZ, 1910

The Fairy Amendments

The powers of fairies are
granted to them to bring
comfort and happiness
to all who appeal to them.

—*Glinda of Oz*, 1920

Fairies cannot be made
invisible against their will.

—*The Lost Princess of Oz*, 1917

Magic must meet magic
in order to conquer it.

—*Glinda of Oz*, 1920

I have lived here many years
and I have not seen
all the wonders
of Oz yet.

—Glinda,
THE SCARECROW
OF OZ, 1915

A Day in the Life of Glinda

A typical day in the life of Glinda goes something like this:

Glinda, the good Sorceress of Oz, gets up early and, after a brisk stroll around her garden, she convenes her royal court where she sits in the grand throne room of her palace, surrounded by her maids of honor—a hundred of the most beautiful girls of the Fairyland of Oz. The palace court is, as you may already know, built of rare marbles, exquisitely polished. Fountains tinkle musically here and there; the vast colonnade, open to the south, allows the maidens, as they raise their heads from their embroideries, to gaze upon a vista of rose-hued fields and groves of trees bearing fruits or laden with sweet-scented flowers. At times one of the girls starts a song, the others join in the chorus, or one stands up to dance, gracefully swaying to the music of a harp played by a companion. And then Glinda smiles, glad to see her maids mixing play with work.

—*GLINDA OF OZ*, 1920

Glinda of Oz

by L. Frank Baum
Illustrated by John R. Neill

The Legal System in Oz

Whenever an appeal is made to law, sorrow
is almost certain to follow—even in a fairyland
like Oz. But it might be stated that the people of
Oz are generally so well behaved that there
is not a single lawyer amongst them.

—*Dorothy and the Wizard in Oz*, 1908

A good many laws seem foolish to those people who
do not understand them, but no law is ever made
without some purpose, and that purpose is usually
to protect all the people and guard their welfare.

—*The Patchwork Girl of Oz*, 1913

No thief, however skillful, can rob one of
knowledge, and that is why knowledge is the
best and safest treasure to acquire.

—*The Lost Princess of Oz*, 1917

Of course, anyone who's sorry just *has* to be forgiven.

—**Dorothy**, *The Lost Princess of Oz*, 1917

I'm in great trouble over the loss of my Magic Belt," declared the King. "Every little while I want to do something magical, and find I can't because the Belt is gone. That makes me angry, and when I'm angry I can't have a good time. Now, what do you advise?"

"Some people," said the Chief Counselor, "enjoy getting angry."

"But not all the time," replied the King. "To be angry once in a while is really good fun, because it makes others so miserable. But to be angry morning, noon and night, as I am, grows monotonous and prevents my gaining any other pleasure in life. Now, what do you advise?"

"Why, if you are angry because you want to do magical

THAT MAKES ME ANGRY!

things and can't, and if you don't want to get angry at all, my advice is not to want to do magical things."

Hearing this, the King glared at his Counselor with a furious expression and tugged at his own long white whiskers until he pulled them so hard that he yelled with pain. "You are a fool!" he exclaimed.

"I share that honor with your Majesty," said the Chief Counselor.

—*THE EMERALD CITY OF OZ*, 1910

40

She Rules Oz

Oz is ruled by Ozma, a real fairy, who is so sweet and gentle in caring for her people that she is greatly beloved by them all. She lives in the most magnificent palace in the most magnificent city in the world, but that does not prevent her from being a true friend to the most humble person in her dominions.

The royal historians of Oz, who are fine writers and know any number of big words, have often tried to describe the rare beauty of Ozma and failed because the words were not good enough. It is said that her loveliness puts to shame all the sparkling jewels and magnificent luxury that surround her in the royal palace. Whatever else is beautiful or dainty or delightful fades to dullness when contrasted with Ozma's bewitching face.

Everything about Ozma inspires love and the sweetest affection rather than awe or ordinary admiration. It is Ozma's custom on her birthday to give herself a grand feast at the palace and invite all her closest friends. This is queerly assorted company, to be sure, for there are more quaint and unusual characters in Oz than in all the rest of the world, and Ozma is more interested in unusual people than in ordinary ones—just as you and I are.

—ADAPTED FROM *THE ROAD TO OZ*, 1909,
AND *THE MAGIC OF OZ*, 1919

In Oz we are loved for our-selves alone, and for our kindness to one another, and for our good deeds.

—**Ozma**, *THE ROAD TO OZ*, 1909

Ruling Class

The Scarecrow was now ruler of the Emerald City, and although he was not a Wizard the people were proud of him. "For," they said, "there is not another city in all the world that is ruled by a stuffed man." And, so far as they knew, they were quite right.

—*The Wonderful Wizard of Oz*, 1900

rincess Langwidere had thirty heads—as many as there are days in the month. But of course she could only wear one of them at a time, because she had but one neck. These heads were kept in what she called her "cabinet," which was a beautiful dressing-room that lay just between her

THIRTY HEADS ARE BETTER THAN ONE

sleeping-chamber and the mirrored sitting room. Each head was in a separate cupboard lined with velvet. The cupboards ran all around the sides of the dressing-room and had elaborately carved doors with gold numbers on the outside and jeweled-framed mirrors inside of them.

When the Princess got out of her crystal bed in the morning she went to her cabinet, opened one of the velvet-lined cupboards, and took the head it

contained from its golden shelf. Then, by the aid of the mirror inside the open door, she put on the head—as neat and straight as could be—and afterward called her maids to robe her for the day. She always wore a simple white costume that suited all the heads. For, being able to change her face whenever she liked, the Princess had no interest in wearing a variety of gowns, as have other ladies who are compelled to wear the same face constantly.

—OZMA OF OZ, 1907

A Grand Title

Like a good many kings and emperors, I have a grand title but very little real power, which allows me time to amuse myself in my own way.

—*The Tin Woodman of Oz*, 1918

An early book review

Impossible as are the little girl's odd companions, the magic pen of the writer, ably assisted by the artist's brush, has made them seem very real, and no child but will have a warm corner in his heart for the really thoughtful Scarecrow, the truly tender Tin Woodman, and the fearless Cowardly Lion. Delightful humor and rare philosophy are found on every page.

—*KINDERGARTEN MAGAZINE*, OCTOBER 1900

Every Road Leads Somewhere

1. Roads in Oz don't go anywhere. They stay in one place so that folks can walk on them.

— *THE ROAD TO OZ, 1909*

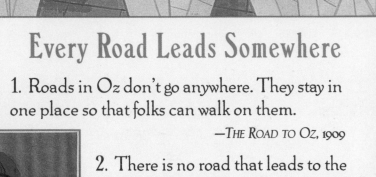

MISS MARGARET HAMBLETON, late of the professional stage, weaves wicked spells and brings to life the wooden man with the pumpkin head in her role as the witch, Mombi, in "The Land of Oz."

2. There is no road that leads to the Wicked Witch of the West. No one ever wants to go there.

— *THE WONDERFUL WIZARD OF OZ, 1900*

3. It's likely that if you travel long enough, you will eventually come to some place or another. What place it will be you can't even guess at the start of your journey, but you're sure to find out once you arrive.

— *THE ROAD TO OZ, 1909*

4. Travelers never take provisions with
them because they know they will be
welcomed wherever they go in the Land
of Oz, and that people will feed and
lodge them with genuine hospitality.

—*THE EMERALD CITY OF OZ, 1910*

5. The road to the
City of Emeralds is paved
with yellow brick, so you
cannot miss it.

—*THE WONDERFUL WIZARD
OF OZ, 1900*

6. Every road leads some-
where or there wouldn't
be a road.

—*THE ROAD TO OZ, 1909*

In the Land of Oz they do not use money at all, every-one is allowed to take what he wishes without price.

—THE MAGIC OF OZ, 1919

AREAS MARKED WITH ARROWS
SHOULD BE PAINTED FIRST.

The Tin Woodman Lectures
on Money in Oz

Money! Money in Oz!" cried the Tin Woodman.
"What a queer idea! Did you suppose we are
so vulgar as to use money here?"

"Why not?" asked the Shaggy Man.

"If we used money to buy things with, instead of
love and kindness and the desire to please one another,
then we should be no better than the rest of the world,"
declared the Tin Woodman. "Fortunately money is
not known in the Land of Oz at all. We have no rich,
and no poor; for what one wishes the others all try to
give him, in order to make him happy, and no one in all
Oz cares to have more than he can use."

—*THE ROAD TO OZ*, 1909

57

Everyone in the Emerald City is happy. They can't help it.
—*The Tin Woodman of Oz*, 1918

The Emerald City:
A Visitor's Guide

I suppose you have read so much about the magnificent Emerald City that there is little need for me to describe it here. It is the Capital City of the Land of Oz, which is justly considered the most attractive and delightful fairyland in the world.

The Emerald City has 9,654 buildings, in which live 47,318 people.

The buildings are constructed of beautiful marbles in which are set masses of emeralds, every one exquisitely cut and of very great size. There are other jewels used in the decorations inside the houses and palaces, such as rubies, diamonds, sapphires, amethysts and turquoises. But in the streets and upon the outside of the buildings only emeralds appear, which is why the place is named the Emerald City of Oz.

The surrounding country, extending to the borders of the desert which enclose it upon every side, is full of pretty and comfortable farmhouses, in which reside those inhabitants of Oz who prefer country to city life.

Altogether there are more than 500,000

people in the Land of Oz—although some of them are not made of flesh and blood as we are. Even without meat on their bones, every inhabitant of that favored country is happy and prosperous.

No disease of any sort exists in Oz, so no one ever gets sick and there are no doctors among them.

There are no poor people in the Land of Oz, because there is no such thing as money, and all property of every sort belongs to the Ruler. The people are her children, and she cares for them. Each person is freely given whatever he requires, which is as much as any one may reasonably desire. Some work the lands and raise great crops of grain, which is divided equally among the entire population, so that everyone can have enough. There are many tailors and dressmakers and shoemakers and the like, who make things that any who desire them can wear. Likewise there are jewelers who make ornaments that please and beautify the people, and these ornaments also are free to those who ask for them.

Each man and woman, no matter what he or she produces for the good of the community, is supplied by the neighbors with food and clothing and a house and furniture and ornaments and games. If by chance the supply ever runs short, more is taken from the great storehouses of the Ruler, which are afterwards filled up again when there is more of any article than the people need.

Everyone works half the time and plays half the time, and the people enjoy their work as much as they do their play, because it is good to be occupied and to have something useful to do. There are no cruel bosses to watch them, and no one to rebuke them or find fault with them. So every worker is proud to do all he can for his friends and neighbors, and is glad when they accept the things he produces.

You will know, by what I have here told you, that the Land of Oz is a remarkable country. I do not suppose such an arrangement would be practical any-where else in the universe, but Dorothy assures us that it works just fine with the Oz people.

Oz being a fairy country, the people are, of course, fairy people; but that does not mean that all of them are very unlike the people of our own world. There are all sorts of queer characters among them, but not a single one who is evil, or who possesses a selfish or violent nature. Otherwise, the inhabitants of Oz are peaceful, kind-hearted, loving and merry, and every inhabitant adores the beautiful girl who rules them, and delights to obey her every command.

In spite of all I have said in a general way, there are some parts of the Land of Oz not quite so pleasant as the farming country and the Emerald City that is its center. Far away

The Emerald City: A Visitor's Guide

in the South Country there lives in the mountains a band of strange people called Hammer-Heads who you'd never want to encounter in a dark alley, or even a well-lit alley, for that matter. They got their name because they have no arms and use their heads to pound anyone who comes near them. Also, in some of the dense forests there live great beasts of every sort; yet even these are for the most part harmless and even sociable, and often willing to converse agreeably with those who visit their haunts. The Kalidahs—beasts with bodies like bears and heads like tigers—are known to have once been fierce and bloodthirsty, but they are now nearly all tamed, although at times one or another of them gets cross and disagreeable and has to be slapped silly by Dorothy or one of her friends.

Not so tame are the Fighting Trees who inhabit a forest of their own. If anyone approaches them, these curious trees bend down their branches, twine them around the intruders, and hurl them away. I've seen this happen and it is not a pretty sight.

But these unpleasant things exist only in a few remote parts of the Land of Oz. I suppose every country has some drawbacks, so even this almost perfect fairyland could not be totally perfect.

The Emerald City: A Visitor's Guide

Perhaps all parts of Oz might not be called truly delightful, but it is surely delightful in the neighborhood of the Emerald City, where Ozma reigns.

Also, when Oz first became a fairyland, it harbored several witches and magicians and sorcerers. These folks were scattered in various parts of the land, but most of them have been either destroyed or deprived of their magic powers. Not long ago, Ozma issued a royal edict forbidding anyone in her dominions to work magic except Glinda the Good and the Wizard of Oz. Ozma herself, being a real fairy, knows a lot of magic, but she only uses it to benefit her subjects.

Another strange thing about this fairy Land of Oz is that whoever manages to enter it from the outside world comes under the magic spell of the place and does not change in appearance as long as they live there. So Dorothy, who now lives with Ozma, seems just the same sweet little girl she was when she first visited this delightful fairyland in the summer of 1899.

—ADAPTED FROM *THE EMERALD CITY OF OZ*, 1910, AND *THE TIN WOODMAN OF OZ*, 1918

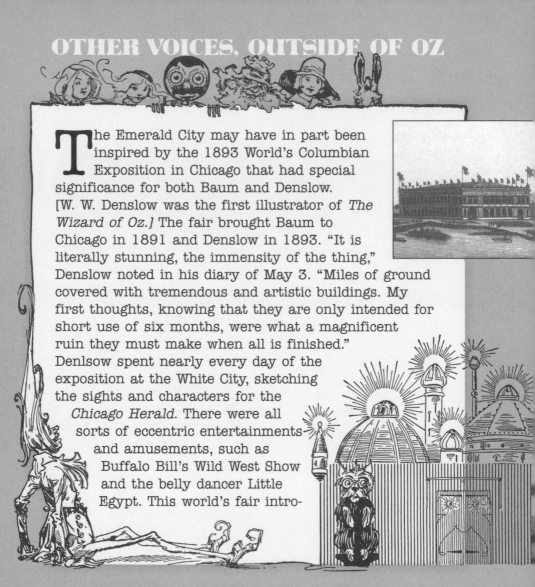

The Emerald City may have in part been inspired by the 1893 World's Columbian Exposition in Chicago that had special significance for both Baum and Denslow. [W. W. Denslow was the first illustrator of *The Wizard of Oz.*] The fair brought Baum to Chicago in 1891 and Denslow in 1893. "It is literally stunning, the immensity of the thing," Denslow noted in his diary of May 3. "Miles of ground covered with tremendous and artistic buildings. My first thoughts, knowing that they are only intended for short use of six months, were what a magnificent ruin they must make when all is finished." Denlsow spent nearly every day of the exposition at the White City, sketching the sights and characters for the *Chicago Herald*. There were all sorts of eccentric entertainments and amusements, such as Buffalo Bill's Wild West Show and the belly dancer Little Egypt. This world's fair intro-

duced cotton candy, Cracker Jack and the Ferris wheel. Like the Emerald City, the White City seemed to spring up suddenly out of nowhere in the center of the country from the swamps along the lake. The shops and vendors along the Midway Pleasance were as lively as those in the capital of Oz. The glittering emeralds may have been suggested by the little lights all over the White City that were lit up at night. . . . Denslow even borrowed the general architecture of the White City, an eclectic blending of European and Near Eastern elements with towers and minarets and banners flying everywhere for the Emerald City.

MICHAEL PATRICK HEARN, THE ANNOTATED WIZARD OF OZ, 2000

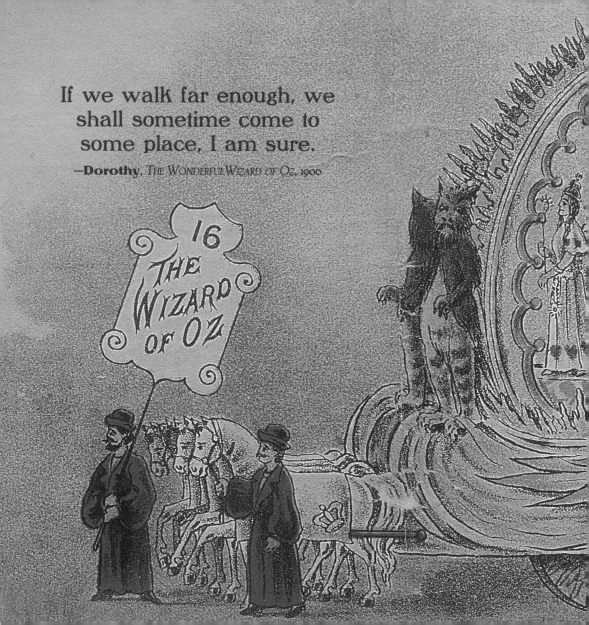

If we walk far enough, we shall sometime come to some place, I am sure.

—**Dorothy**, *The Wonderful Wizard of Oz*, 1900

Actual listing in the TV section of the *Marin Independent-Journal*, Marin, California, Summer, 2002:

Movie "The Wizard of Oz": Transported to a surreal landscape, a young girl kills the first woman she meets, then teams up with three complete strangers to kill again.

Magical Places

I grew up in southern California, far from Oz—or even Kansas, for that matter. But it made no difference. Magical places have their own logic. There was always a chance I might find my way there. Trudging toward school on Monday morning I had my eyes peeled.

—MARK TEAGUE, *OZ/THE HUNDREDTH ANNIVERSARY CELEBRATION*, 2000

You Have to Ask

If one does not ask for information he seldom receives it; so I, for my part, make it a rule to answer any civil question that is asked me.

—*The Tin Woodman of Oz*, 1918

A Wogglebug Education

I had the College of Art and Athletic Perfection built quite recently," said Ozma. "The young students who attend the college are no worse off than they were before. You see, in this country there are a number of youths who do not like to work, and the college is an excellent place for them."

The college is located in the Munchkin Country, not far from the Emerald City. Professor H. M. Wogglebug, T. E., is the Principal. To enable the students to devote all their time to athletic exercises, the Professor invented an assortment of Tablets of Learning. One of these tablets, eaten by a student after breakfast, instantly enables him or her to understand arithmetic or algebra or any other branch of mathematics. Another tablet eaten after lunch gives a student a complete knowledge of geography. Another tablet makes it possible for the diner to spell the most difficult words and still another enables him to recite poems. There are tablets for history, language, and science and it doesn't matter whether a boy or a girl is stupid or brilliant, for the tablets teach them everything in the twinkling of an eye.

This method, which is patented in the Land of Oz by Professor Wogglebug, saves paper and books, as well as the tedious hours devoted to study in some of our less favored schools. More importantly, it also allows the students to devote all their time to baseball,

A Wogglebug Education

racing, tennis and other manly and womanly sports which are greatly interfered with by study in those Temples of Learning where Tablets of Learning are unknown.

Unfortunately, it so happened that Professor Wogglebug (who had invented so much that he had acquired the habit) carelessly invented a Square-Meal Tablet, which was no bigger than your little fingernail but contained, in condensed form, the equal of a bowl of tomato soup, a portion of broccoli, a slice of roast beef, a salad and a slice of chocolate cake, all of which gave the same nourishment as a square meal.

The Professor was so proud of these Square-Meal Tablets that he began to feed them to the students at his college, instead of other food, but the boys and girls objected because they wanted food that they could enjoy the taste of. It was no fun at all to swallow a tablet, with a glass of water, and call it dinner; so they refused to eat the Square-Meal Tablets. Professor Wogglebug insisted, and the result was that the Senior Class seized the learned Professor one day and threw him into the river—clothes and all. Everyone knows that a wogglebug cannot swim, and so the inventor of the wonderful Square-Meal Tablets lay helpless on the bottom of the river for three days before a fisherman caught one of his legs on a fishhook and dragged him out upon the bank.

The learned Professor was naturally indignant at such treatment, and so he brought the entire Senior Class to the Emerald City and appealed to Ozma of Oz to punish them for their rebellion.

The girl Ruler was very lenient with the rebellious boys and girls because she had herself refused to eat the Square-Meal Tablets in place of food.

—*The Magic of Oz*, 1919

I once knew a little boy who wanted to catch the measles," Dorothy said, "because all the little boys in his neighborhood but him had had 'em, and he was really unhappy 'cause he couldn't catch 'em, try as he would. So I'm pretty certain that the things we want, and can't have, are not good for us. Isn't that true, Shaggy?"

THE WISDOM OF THE SHAGGY MAN

"Not always, my dear," he gravely replied. "If we didn't want anything, we would never get anything, good or bad. I think our longings are natural, and if we act as nature prompts us we can't go far wrong."

"For my part," said Queen Ann, "I think the world would be a dreary place without the gold and jewels."

"All things are good in their way," said Shaggy; "but we may have too much of any good thing. And I have noticed that the value of anything depends upon how scarce it is, and how difficult it is to obtain."

—TIK-TOK OF OZ, 1914

The Best Thinker

The best thinker I ever knew," said Dorothy to the yellow hen, "was a scarecrow."

"Nonsense!" snapped Billina.

"It is true," declared Dorothy. "I met him in the Land of Oz, and he traveled with me to the city of the great Wizard of Oz, so as to get some brains, for his head was only stuffed with straw. But it seemed to me that he thought just as well before he got his brains as he did afterward."

—OZMA OF OZ, 1907

82

It is such an
uncomfortable feeling
to know you are a fool.

—**Scarecrow**, *The Wonderful Wizard of Oz*, 1900

WHEN SEATED AT YOUR
DON'T SLUMP DO

like the "**PATCHWORK GIRL**"

These quaint characters are quoted from the famous Oz Books and were created by L. Frank Baum. Used by permission of Reilly & Lee Company, the publishers.

OR

the "S

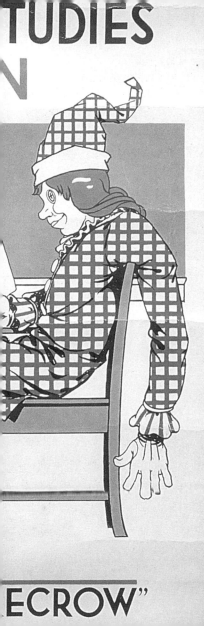

STUDIES
N

ECROW"

A Quiet Think

"And now I will indulge in a quiet think," said the Scarecrow.

The others remained as silent and still as possible, so as not to disturb him; for all had great confidence in the extraordinary brains of the Scarecrow.

—*THE MARVELOUS LAND OF OZ*, 1904

Many Brains

"If a few brains are good, many brains must be better."

—*THE PATCHWORK GIRL OF OZ*, 1913

Sweet, Fresh, Golden Straw:
The Scarecrow's Anthem

What sound is so sweet
As the straw from the wheat
When it crunkles so
   tender and low?
It is yellow and bright,
So it gives me delight
To crunkle wherever I go.

Sweet, fresh, golden Straw!
There is surely no flaw
In a stuffing so clean and
   compact.
It creaks when I walk,
And it thrills when I talk,
And its fragrance is fine, for a fact.

To cut me don't hurt,
For I've no blood to squirt,

And I therefore can suffer no pain;
The straw that I use
Doesn't lump or bruise,
Though it's pounded
again and again!

I know it is said
That my beautiful head
Has brains of mixed wheat-
straw and bran,
But my thoughts are so good
I'd not change, if I could,
For the brains of a common
meat man.

Content with my lot,
I'm glad that I'm not
Like others I meet day by day;
If my insides get musty,
Or mussed-up, or dusty,
I get newly stuffed right away.

—THE TIN WOODMAN OF OZ, 1918

Read This Tree

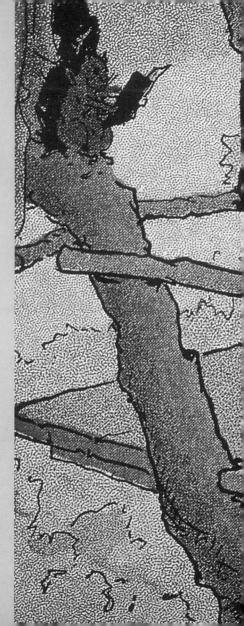

The most interesting flora and fauna are grown in Oz by Jo Files, a young man and tree farmer. Files has twelve trees on which grow steel files of various sorts; but he also has nine book-trees, on which grow a choice selection of story books.

In case you've never seen books growing upon trees, I will explain that those in Jo Files' orchard are enclosed in broad green husks which, when fully ripe, turn a deep red color. Then the books are picked and husked and ready to read. If picked too soon, the stories are confusing and uninteresting and the spelling bad. However, if allowed to ripen perfectly, the stories are fine reading with excellent grammar and interesting plot lines.

Files freely gives his books to anyone who wants them, but the people of his village care little for books and so he has to read most of them himself, before they spoil. For, as you probably know, as soon as the books are read the words disappear and the leaves wither and fade—which is the worst fault of all books which grow upon trees.

—*TIK-TOK OF OZ*, 1914

D orothy was hungry. All alone in the woods, without a house in sight, she decided to search for nuts or berries in the woods. At first she was greatly disappointed, because the nearer trees were all cottonwood or eucalyptus, and bore no fruit or nuts at all. But, bye and bye, when she was almost in despair, the little girl came upon two trees that promised to furnish her with plenty of food.

One was quite full of square paper boxes which grew in clusters on all the limbs, and upon the biggest and ripest boxes the word "Lunch" could be read, in neatly raised letters. This tree seemed to flower all the year around, for there were lunch-box blossoms on some of the branches and on others tiny little lunch-boxes that were as yet quite green, and evidently not fit to eat until they had grown bigger.

THE LUNCH-BOX TREE

The leaves of this tree were all paper napkins, and it presented a very pleasing appearance to the hungry little girl.

THE LUNCH-BOX TREE

But the tree next to the lunch-box tree was even more wonderful, for it bore quantities of tin dinner pails, which were so full and heavy that the stout branches bent underneath their weight.

Some were small and dark-brown in color; those larger were of a dull tin color; but the really ripe ones were pails of bright tin that shone and glistened beautifully in the rays of sunshine that touched them.

Dorothy was delighted. She stood on tip-toe and picked one of the nicest and biggest lunch-boxes and then she sat down upon the ground and eagerly opened it. Inside she found, nicely wrapped in white paper, a ham sandwich, a piece of chocolate cake, a pickle, a slice of American cheese and an apple. Each thing had a separate stem, and so had to be picked off the side of the box; but Dorothy found them all to be delicious, and she ate every bit of lunch in the box.

—OZMA OF OZ, 1907

95

Dining in Oz

No one starves in the Land of Oz. There is plenty for everyone, you know; only, if it isn't just where you happen to be, you must go where it is.
—*THE PATCHWORK GIRL OF OZ*, 1904

People do not eat chickens here. You see, Billina was the first hen that was ever seen in this country, and Dorothy brought her here herself. Everybody liked the yellow hen and respected her, so the Oz people wouldn't any more eat her chickens than they would eat Billina.
—*THE EMERALD CITY OF OZ*, 1910

No one ever starved to death in Oz, but people get pretty hungry sometimes.
—*THE EMERALD CITY OF OZ*, 1910

My mouth is painted on and there's no swallow connected to it.
—**Scarecrow**, *THE LAND OF OZ*, 1904

I never eat because
I am stuffed full already, and
I like my nice clean straw
better than I do food.

—**Scarecrow**, *The Scarecrow of Oz*, 1915

The Hungry Tiger

You can hardly imagine the size of my appetite," said the Tiger, sadly. "It seems to fill my whole body, from the end of my throat to the tip of my tail. I am very sure my appetite doesn't fit me, and is too large for the size of my body. Someday, when I meet a dentist with a pair of forceps, I am going to have it pulled."

"What, your tooth?" asked Dorothy.

"No, my appetite," said the Hungry Tiger.

—*Ozma of Oz*, 1907

The Cowardly Lion and the Hungry Tiger

In the splendid palace of the Emerald City, which is in the center of the Fairy Land of Oz, is a great Throne Room, where Princess Ozma, the Ruler, for an hour each day sits in a throne of glistening emeralds and listens to all the troubles of her people. Around Ozma's throne, on such occasions, are grouped all the important personages of Oz, and crouched on either side of the throne are two enormous beasts known as the Hungry Tiger and the Cowardly Lion.

These two beasts are Ozma's chief guardians, but as everyone loves the beautiful girl Princess there has never been any disturbance in the great Throne Room, or anything for the guardians to do but look fierce and solemn and keep quiet until the Royal Audience is over and the people return to their homes.

Of course no one would dare be naughty while the huge Lion and Tiger crouched beside the throne; but the fact is, the people of Oz are very seldom naughty. So Ozma's big guards are more ornamental than useful, and no one realizes that better than the beasts themselves.

One day, after everybody had left the Throne Room except the Cowardly Lion and the Hungry Tiger, the Lion yawned and said to his friend, "I'm getting tired of this job. No one is afraid of us and no one pays any attention to us."

"That is true," replied

the big Tiger, purring softly. "We might as well be in the thick jungles where we were born, as trying to protect Ozma when she needs no protection. And I'm dreadfully hungry all the time."

"You have enough to eat, I'm sure," said the Lion.

"Enough, perhaps; but not the kind of food I long for," answered the Tiger. "What I'm hungry for is fat babies. I have a great desire to eat a few fat babies. Then, perhaps, the people of Oz would fear me and I'd become more important."

"True," agreed the Lion. "It would stir up quite a scare if you ate but one fat baby. As for myself, my claws are sharp as needles and strong as crowbars, while my teeth are powerful enough to tear a person to pieces in a few seconds. If I should spring upon a man and make chop suey of him, there would be wild excitement in the Emerald City and the people would fall upon their knees and beg me for mercy. That, in my opinion, would render me of considerable importance."

"After you had torn the person to pieces, what would you do next?" asked the Tiger sleepily.

"I would roar so loudly it would shake the earth and stalk away to the jungle to hide myself, before anyone could attack me or kill me for what I had done."

"I see," nodded the Tiger. "You are really cowardly."

"That is why I am named the Cowardly Lion and why I have always been so tame and peaceable. But I'm awfully tired of being tame," added the Lion, with

a sigh, "and it would be fun to show people what a terrible beast I really am."

The Tiger remained silent for several minutes, thinking as he slowly washed his face with his left paw. Then he said, "I'm getting old, and it would please me to eat at least one fat baby before I die. Suppose we surprise these people of Oz and prove our power. We'll walk out of here just as usual and the first baby we meet I'll eat in a jiffy, and the first man or woman you meet you'll tear to pieces. Then we'll both run out of the city gates and gallop across the country and hide in the jungle before anyone can stop us."

"I'm game," said the Lion, yawning again so that he showed two rows of dreadfully sharp teeth.

The Tiger got up and stretched his great, sleek body. "Come on," he said.

The Lion stood up and proved he was the larger of the two, for he was almost as big as a small horse.

Out of the palace they walked, and met no one. They passed through the beautiful grounds, past fountains and beds of lovely flowers, and met no one. Then they unlatched a gate and entered a street of the city, and met no one.

"I wonder how a fat baby will taste," remarked the Tiger, as they stalked majestically along, side by side.

"I imagine it will taste like nutmeg," said the Lion.

"No," said the Tiger, "I've an idea it will taste like gumdrops."

They turned a corner, but met no one, for the people of the Emerald City were accustomed to taking their naps at this hour of the afternoon.

"I wonder how many pieces I should tear a person into," said the Lion, in a thoughtful voice.

"Sixty would be about right," suggested the Tiger.

"Would that hurt any more than to

tear one into about a dozen pieces?" asked the Lion, with a little shudder.

"Who cares whether it hurts or not?" growled the Tiger.

The Lion did not reply. As they entered a side street, suddenly they heard a child crying.

"Aha!" exclaimed the Tiger. "There is my meat."

He rushed around a corner, the Lion following, and came upon a nice fat baby sitting in the middle of the street and crying as if in great distress.

"What's the matter?" asked the Tiger, crouching before the baby.

"I—I—I—lost my m-m-mommy!" wailed the baby.

"Why, you poor little thing," said the great beast, softly stroking the child's head with its paw. "Don't cry, my dear, for mommy can't be far away and I'll help you find her."

"Go on," said the Lion, who stood by.

"Go on where?" asked the Tiger, looking up.

"Go on and eat your fat baby."

"Why, you dreadful creature!" said the Tiger. "Would you want me to eat a poor little lost baby, that doesn't know where its mother is?" And the beast gathered the little one into its strong, hairy arms and tried to comfort it by rocking it gently back and forth.

The Lion growled low in his throat and seemed very much disappointed. At that moment a scream reached their ears and a woman came bounding out of a house and into the street. Seeing her baby in the embrace of the monster Tiger the woman screamed again and rushed forward to rescue it, but in her haste she caught her foot in her skirt and tumbled head over heels and heels over head, stopping with such a bump that she saw many stars in the heavens, although it was broad daylight. And there she helplessly lay, all tangled up and unable to stir.

With one bound and a roar like thunder, the huge Lion was beside her. With his strong jaws he grasped her dress and raised her into an upright position. "Poor thing! Are you hurt?" he gently asked.

Gasping for breath the woman struggled to free herself and tried to walk, but she limped badly and tumbled down again.

"My baby!" she said pleadingly.

"The baby is all right; don't worry," replied the Lion; and then he added: "Keep quiet, now, and I'll carry you back to your house, and the Hungry Tiger will carry your baby."

The Tiger, who had approached the place with the child in its arms, asked, "Aren't you going to tear her into sixty pieces?"

"No, nor into six pieces," answered the Lion. "I'm not such a brute as to destroy a poor woman who has hurt herself trying to save her lost baby. If you are so ferocious and cruel and bloodthirsty, you may leave me and go away, for I do not care to associate with you."

"That's all right," answered the Tiger. "I'm not cruel—not in the least—I'm only hungry. But I thought you were cruel."

"Thank heaven I'm respectable," said the Lion, with dignity. He then raised the woman and with much gentleness carried her into her house, where he laid her upon a sofa. The Tiger followed with the baby, which he safely deposited beside its mother. The little one liked the Hungry Tiger and grasping the enormous beast by both ears the baby kissed the beast's nose to show he was grateful and happy.

"Thank you very much," said the

woman. "I've often heard what good beasts you are, in spite of your power to do mischief to mankind, and now I know that the stories are true. I do not think either of you have ever had an evil thought."

The Hungry Tiger and the Cowardly Lion hung their heads and did not look into each other's eyes, for both were shamed and humbled. They crept away and stalked back through the streets until they again entered the palace grounds, where they retreated to the pretty, comfortable rooms they occupied at the back of the palace. There they silently crouched in their usual corners to think over their adventure.

After a while the Tiger said sleepily: "I don't believe fat babies taste like gumdrops. I'm quite sure they have the flavor of raspberry tarts. My, how hungry I am for fat babies!"

The Lion grunted disdainfully. "You're a humbug," said he.

"Am I?" retorted the Tiger, with a sneer. "Tell me, then, into how many pieces you usually tear your victims, my bold Lion?"

The Lion impatiently thumped the floor with his tail. "To tear anyone into pieces would soil my claws and blunt my teeth," he said. "I'm glad I didn't muss myself up this afternoon by hurting that poor mother."

The Tiger looked at him steadily. "You're a coward," he remarked.

"Well," said the Lion, "it's better to be a coward than to do wrong."

"To be sure," answered the other. "And that reminds me that I nearly lost my own reputation. For, had I eaten that fat baby, I would not now be the Hungry Tiger. It's better to go hungry, seems to me, than to be cruel to a little child."

And then they dropped their heads on their paws and went to sleep.

—*Little Wizard Stories,* 1914

Animal Life in Oz

In Oz, where all the animals and birds can talk,
many fishes are able to talk also, but usually they
are more stupid than birds and animals because
they think slowly and haven't much to talk about.

—*GLINDA OF OZ*, 1920

"We have some very large mosquitoes here in Oz, which
sing as beautifully as song birds," said the Tin Woodman.
"But they never bite or annoy our people, because they
are well fed and taken care of. The reason they bite
people on earth is because they are hungry—poor things!"

—*THE EMERALD CITY OF OZ*, 1910

There is nothing in the world quite so
miserable as a wet hen.

—*OZMA OF OZ*, 1907

Neither boys nor monkeys relish being scrubbed.

—*THE TIN WOODMAN OF OZ*, 1918

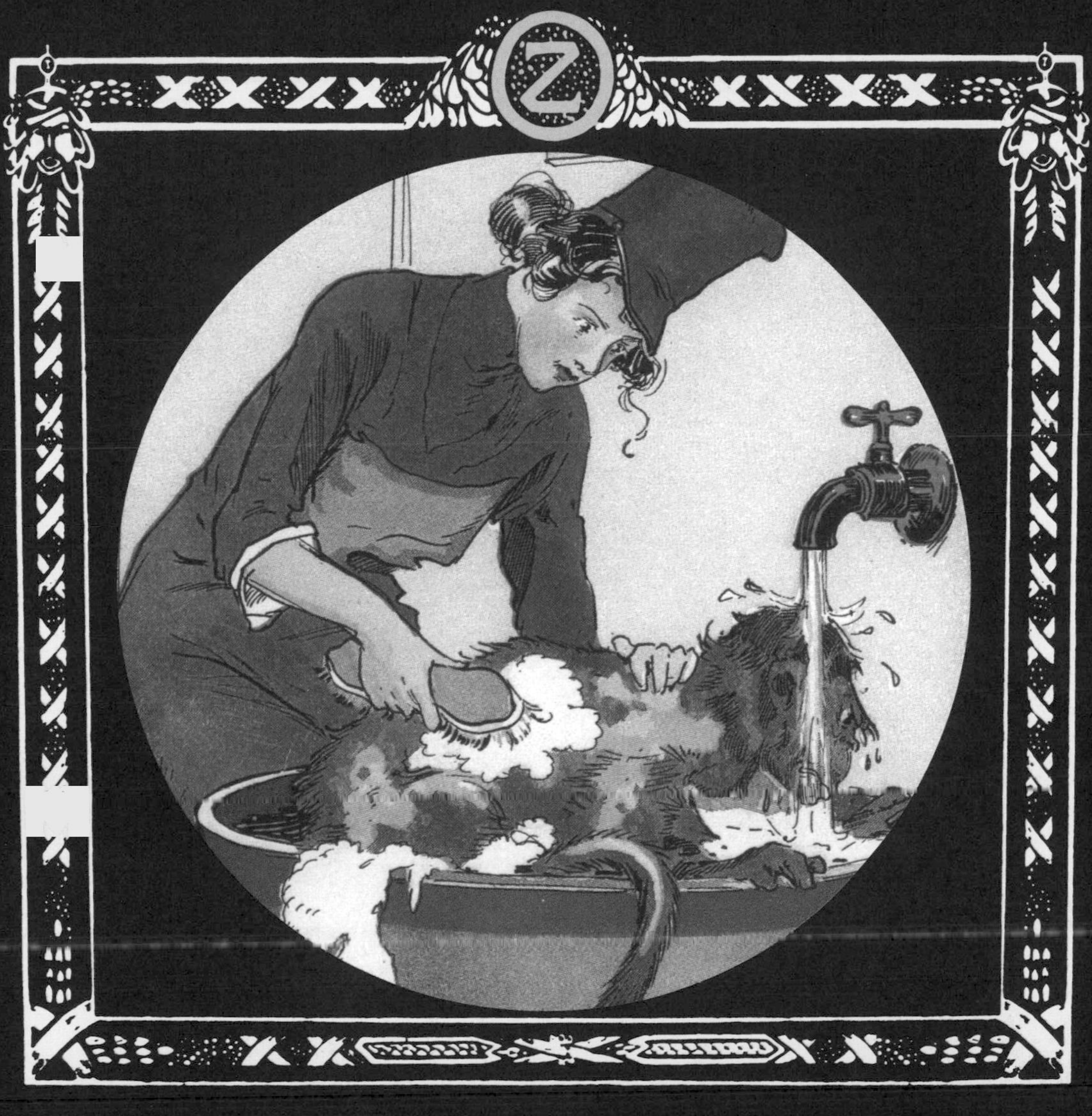

Now the charm began to work. The sky was
darkened, and a low rumbling sound was heard
in the air. There was a rushing of many wings; a
great chattering and laughing; and the sun came out of
the dark sky to show the Wicked Witch surrounded
by a crowd of Monkeys, each with a pair of immense
and powerful wings on his shoulders.

—*THE WONDERFUL WIZARD OF OZ*, 1900

A Crowd
of Monkeys

Watching the Movie

While watching the movie *The Wizard of Oz* I found the flying monkeys swooping down on the heroes graceful, scary, and unforgettable. For years after, I was sure that they would come into the dark bedroom and lift me, bed and all, and carry me away. Not through the window, which was too small, but exploding through the roof. Never mind that old Mrs. Mersant lived upstairs, and that bed, boy, and beasts would have to crash through her floor and ceiling on our way to the castle of the Wicked Witch of the West. Those flying monkeys couldn't be stopped.

—BRUCE DEGEN, *OZ/THE HUNDREDTH ANNIVERSARY CELEBRATION*, 2000

The Woggle Bug Song

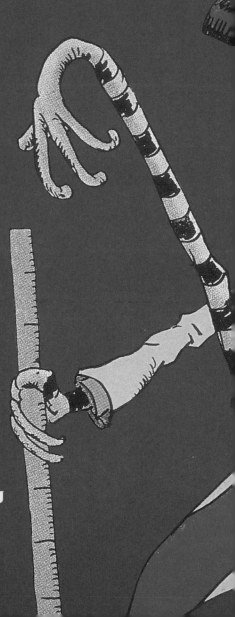

I appear as rather queer,
You needn't fear to stare
Though I am quite a novel sight
I'm very well aware
Though not a freak
I'm so to speak
Of most unique design
Despite my size
I'm wondrous wise
And bound to cut a shine
And then I guess
You will confess
My gorgeous dress is fine.

For I'm Mister H. M. Woggle Bug
There's a charm about my style
Makes the lady beatles smile

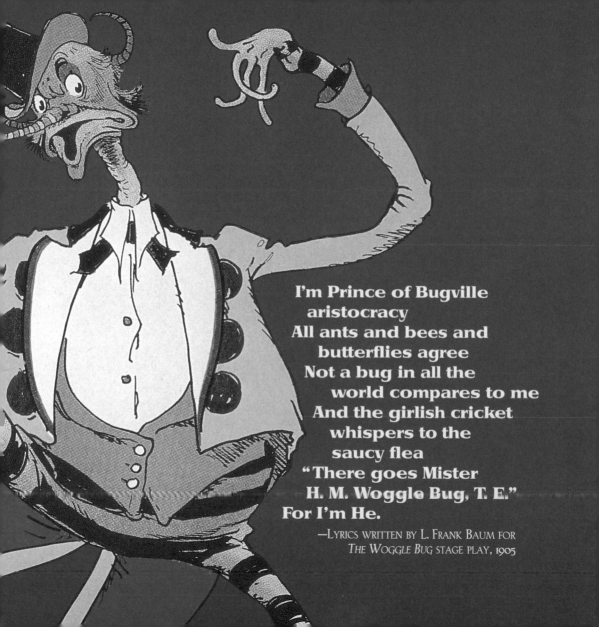

I'm Prince of Bugville
aristocracy
All ants and bees and
butterflies agree
Not a bug in all the
world compares to me
And the girlish cricket
whispers to the
saucy flea
"There goes Mister
H. M. Woggle Bug, T. E."
For I'm He.

—Lyrics written by L. Frank Baum for
The Woggle Bug stage play, 1905

The Only Dog in Oz

Toto did not really care whether he
was in Kansas or the Land of Oz so
long as Dorothy was with him.
—*THE WONDERFUL WIZARD OF OZ, 1900*

Being the only dog in the Land of Oz,
Toto was highly respected by the people, who
believed animals were entitled to every consideration if they behaved themselves properly.
—*THE EMERALD CITY OF OZ, 1910*

Song of the Fishes

We are the fishes of the lake;
Our lives are very deep;
We're always active when awake
And quiet when asleep.

We get our fins from Finland,
From books we get our tales;
Our eyes come from old England
And weighty are our scales.

We love to flop, to twist and turn
Whenever 'tis our whim;
Yet social etiquette we learn
Because we're in the swim.

Our beds, though damp,
   are always made;
We need no fires to warm us;
When we swim out
   we're not afraid,
For autos cannot harm us.

We're independent little fish
And never use umbrellas.
We do exactly as we wish
And live like jolly fellows.

—Poem by L. Frank Baum published in
L. Frank Baum's Juvenile Speaker, 1910

123

Is the Scarecrow Alive, Grasshopper?

Oh! Are you alive?" asked the grasshopper.

"That is a question I have never been able to decide," said the Scarecrow's head. "When my body is properly stuffed I have animation and can move around as well as any live person. The brains in the head you are now occupying as a throne, are of very superior quality and do a lot of very clever thinking. But whether that is being alive, or not, I cannot prove to you; for one who lives is liable to death, while I am only liable to destruction."

—*THE SCARECROW OF OZ*, 1915

Pity the Poor Meat People

I feel much better now that my joints are oiled," said the Tin Woodman, with a sigh of pleasure. "You and I, friend Scarecrow, are much more easily cared for than those clumsy meat people, who spend half their time dressing in fine clothes and who must live in splendid dwellings in order to be happy. You and I do not eat, and so we are spared the dreadful bother of getting three meals a day. Nor do we waste half our lives in sleep, a condition that causes the meat people to lose all consciousness and become as thoughtless and helpless as logs of wood."

—*The Lost Princess of Oz*, 1917

Birds Are the Luckiest Creatures of All

I often feel sorry for the meat people, many of whom are my friends," said the Scarecrow. "Even the beasts are happier than they, for they require less to make them content. And the birds are the luckiest creatures of all, for they can fly swiftly where they will and find a home at any place they care to perch; their food consists of seeds and grains they gather from the field and their drink is a sip of water from some running brook. If I could not be a Scarecrow or a Tin Woodman, my next choice would be to live as a bird does."

—*The Lost Princess of Oz*, 1917

GLOBE THEATRE BOSTON
Weeks Jan. 28 - Feb. 4
MATS—MON. WED. SAT.

I've heard that anyone can be

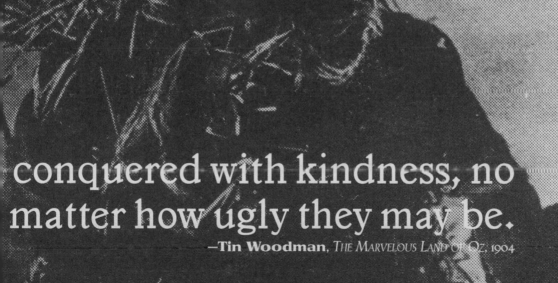

conquered with kindness, no matter how ugly they may be.

—**Tin Woodman**, *The Marvelous Land of Oz*, 1904

Military Life in Oz

"I have in my Army eight Generals," said the Tin Woodman, "six Colonels, seven Majors and five Captains, besides one private for them to command. I'd like to promote the private, for I believe no private should ever be in public life."

—*OZMA OF OZ*, 1907

The way to conquer is to act, and he
who acts promptly is sure to win.

—*THE LOST PRINCESS OF OZ*, 1917

"Girls are the fiercest soldiers of all," declared
the Frogman. "They are more brave than men
and they have better nerves."

—*THE LOST PRINCESS OF OZ*, 1917

The Generals commanded the Colonels and the Colonels
commanded the Majors and the Majors commanded
the Captains and the Captains commanded the Private,
who marched with an air of proud importance because
it required so many officers to give him orders.

—*OZMA OF OZ*, 1907

An unsuspected
enemy is doubly
dangerous.

—*The Emerald City
of Oz*, 1910

A Means of Escape

W ell," said the Scarecrow, after a moment's thought, "I don't mind much the loss of my throne, for it's a tiresome job to rule over the Emerald City. And this crown is so heavy that it makes my head ache. But I hope the Conquerors have no intention of injuring me, just because I happen to be the King."

"I heard them say," remarked Tip, with some hesitation, "that they intend to make a rag carpet of your outside and stuff their sofacushions with your inside."

"Then I am really in danger," declared his Majesty, positively, "and it will be wise for me to consider a means of escape."

—*THE MARVELOUS LAND OF OZ*, 1904

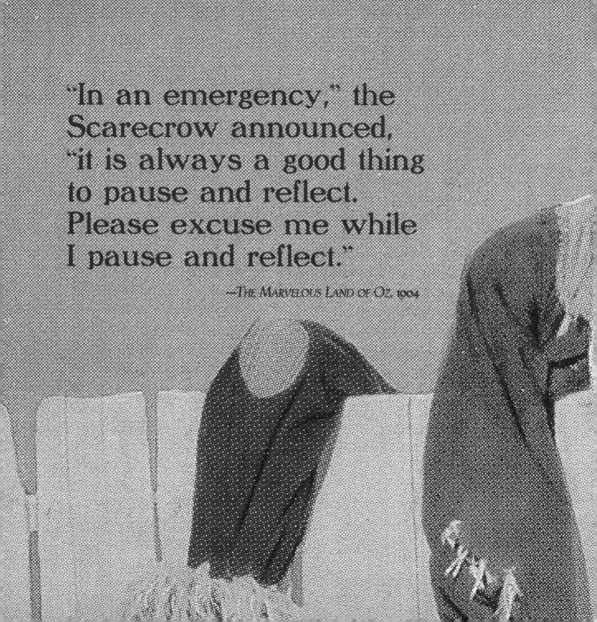

"In an emergency," the Scarecrow announced, "it is always a good thing to pause and reflect. Please excuse me while I pause and reflect."

—The Marvelous Land of Oz, 1904

おくびょうなライオン

「サルみたいなとりよ！」
「とりみたいなサルだ！」
いままでみたこともない
かいぶつのしゅうげきに、
ドロシーたちは、うろうろ
するばかりでした。

The Tin Woodman
is usually a peaceful
man, but when
occasion requires he
can fight as fiercely as
a Roman gladiator.

—*The Marvelous Land of Oz*, 1904

Favorite Sayings in Oz

Be contented with your fate, for discontent
leads to unhappiness, and unhappiness, in any
form, is the greatest evil that can befall you.

—*THE TIN WOODMAN OF OZ*, 1918

Cruel people are always cowards.

—*THE SCARECROW OF OZ*, 1915

When we try to deceive people,
we always make mistakes.

—*THE EMERALD CITY OF OZ*, 1910

Always when there's trouble, there's a
way out of it, if you can find it.

—*THE LOST PRINCESS OF OZ*, 1917

We all have our weaknesses, dear friends; so
we must strive to be considerate of one another.

—*THE MARVELOUS LAND OF OZ*, 1904

Friends must stand together!
—*THE SCARECROW OF OZ*, 1915

People often do a good deed
without hope of reward, but
for an evil deed they always
demand payment.
—*THE EMERALD CITY OF OZ*, 1910

Kings aren't always popular
with their people, you know,
even if they do the best
they know how.
—*THE SCARECROW OF OZ*, 1915

Laughter is the best
thing in life.
—*THE PATCHWORK GIRL OF OZ*, 1913

Come along, Toto. We shall go to the Emerald City and ask the great Oz how to get back to Kansas again.

—**Dorothy**, *The Wonderful Wizard of Oz*, 1900

I believe it is wrong to worry over anything before it happens.

—**Scarecrow**, *The Emerald City of Oz*, 1910

They ain't no word in the booktionary to describe us.

—**Cap'n Bill**, *The Scarecrow of Oz*, 1915

Conceptions of Earth

It occurs to me that my most vivid conceptions of Earth come from the Oz stories—and when you come down to it, I suppose that isn't too reliable a source. I mean, Dorothy's conversations with the Wizard are instructive—but about *what*? When I was a child I believed every word of my Oz tapes; but now I am no longer a child and I do not truly suppose that a whirlwind is a reliable means of transportation, nor that one is likely to encounter a Tin Woodman on a road of yellow brick.

—Robert A. Heinlein, *Podkayne of Mars*, 1963

The more you fish for what you want, the less chance you have of getting it.

—**Scarecrow**, *THE MARVELOUS LAND OF OZ*, 1904

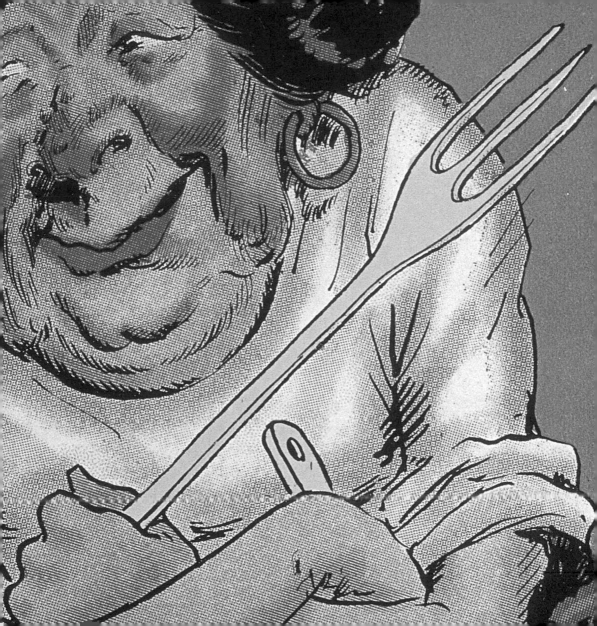

"The Wizard of Oz"

Writing Fairy Stories

To write fairy stories for children, to amuse them, to divert restless children, sick children, to keep them out of mischief on rainy days, seems of greater importance than to write grown-up novels. Few of the popular novels last the year out, responding as they do to a certain psychological demand characteristic of the time; whereas, a child's book is, comparatively speaking, the same always, since children are always the same kind of folks with the same needs to be satisfied.

—L. FRANK BAUM,
THE GRAND RAPIDS HERALD,
AUGUST 18, 1907

Girl Power

It was lucky for Dorothy, I think, that the storm subsided; otherwise, brave though she was, I fear she might have perished. Many children, in her place, would have wept and given way to despair; but because Dorothy had encountered so many adventures and come safely through them it did not occur to her at this time to be especially afraid. She was wet and uncomfortable, it is true; but, after sighing one sigh, she managed to recall some of her customary cheerfulness and decided to patiently await whatever her fate might be.

—OZMA OF OZ, 1907

154

What Should We Do Next?

Of course Toto made for Dorothy at once, barking joyfully the moment he was released. When the child had patted Toto's head lovingly, he sat down before her, his red tongue hanging out one side of his mouth, and looked up into her face with his bright brown eyes, as if asking her what they should do next.

—*THE ROAD TO OZ*, 1909

Never give up.
No one knows
what's going to
happen next.

—**Dorothy**, *THE PATCHWORK GIRL OF OZ*, 1913

Some Movies Never Die

From underwear to marshmallows, wall masks to thimbles, cake decorating kits to lithographs and porcelain figurines of a Cowardly Lion, a Tin Woodman, and a small dog, hundreds of different products have accompanied the *The Wizard of Oz* [movie] into its sixtieth year. We live in a world where almost everything can be bought or sold. And commerce has its place. But, at its heart, the yellow brick road is beyond commerce. I envy the children who have yet to see *The Wizard of Oz* for the first time.

—ALJEAN HARMETZ, *THE MAKING OF THE WIZARD OF OZ*, 1977

When we have the least
reason for getting into
trouble, something is
sure to go wrong.

—THE TIN WOODMAN OF OZ, 1918

"HALT!"

A Visit to Utensil Town

Dorothy, Toto and Billina the Hen were walking in the woods one beautiful afternoon when suddenly a voice cried sharply:

"Halt!"

At first Dorothy could see nothing, although she looked around very carefully. But Billina exclaimed:

"Well, I declare!"

"What is it?" asked the little girl: for Toto began barking at something, and following his gaze she discovered what it was.

A row of spoons had surrounded the three, and these spoons stood straight up on their handles and carried swords and muskets. Their faces were outlined in the polished bowls and they looked very stern and severe.

Dorothy laughed at the queer things. "Who are you?" she asked.

"We're the Spoon Brigade," said one.

"In the service of his Majesty King Kleaver," said another.

"And you are our prisoners," said a third.

Dorothy sat down on an old stump and looked at them, her eyes twinkling with amusement.

"What would happen," she inquired, "if I should set my dog on your Brigade?"

"He would die," replied one of the spoons, sharply. "One shot from our deadly muskets would kill him, big as he is."

A Visit to Utensil Town

"Don't risk it, Dorothy," advised the Yellow Hen. "Remember this is a fairy country, yet none of us three happens to be a fairy."

Dorothy grew sober at this.

"Maybe you're right, Billina," she answered. "But how funny it is, to be captured by a lot of spoons!"

"I don't see anything very funny about it," declared a spoon. "We're the regular military Brigade of the kingdom."

"What kingdom?" she asked.

"Utensil Town," said he.

"I never heard of it before," asserted Dorothy.

"We are subjects of King Kleaver," returned the spoon, "and obey only his orders, which are to bring all prisoners to him as soon as they are captured. So step lively, my girl, and march with us, or we may be tempted to cut off a few of your toes with our swords."

This threat made Dorothy laugh again. She did not believe she was in any danger; but here was a new and interesting adventure, so she was willing to be taken to Utensil Town that she might see what King Kleaver's kingdom was like.

There must have been from six to

A Visit to Utensil Town

eight dozen spoons in the Brigade, and they marched away in the shape of a hollow square, with Dorothy, Billina and Toto in the center of the square. Before they had gone very far Toto knocked over one of the spoons by wagging his tail, and then the Captain of the Spoons told the little dog to be more careful, or he would be punished. So Toto was careful, and the Spoon Brigade moved along with astonishing swiftness, while Dorothy really had to walk fast to keep up with it.

By and by they left the woods and entered a big clearing, in which was the Kingdom of Utensil Town.

Standing all around the clearing were a good many cook-stoves, ranges and grills, of all sizes and shapes, and besides these there were several kitchen cabinets and cupboards and a few kitchen tables. These things were crowded with utensils of all sorts: frying pans, sauce pans, kettles, forks, knives, basting and soup spoons, nutmeg graters, sifters, colanders, meat saws, flat irons, rolling pins and many other things of a like nature.

When the Spoon Brigade appeared with the prisoners a wild shout arose and many of the utensils hopped off their stoves or their benches and ran crowding around Dorothy and the hen and the dog.

"Stand back!" cried the Captain, sternly, and he led his captives through the curious throng until they came before a big range that stood in the center of the clearing. Beside this range was a butcher's block upon which lay a great cleaver with a keen edge. It rested upon the flat of its back, its legs were crossed and it was smoking a long pipe.

"Wake up, your Majesty," said the Captain. "Here are prisoners."

Hearing this, King Kleaver sat up and looked at Dorothy sharply.

A Visit to Utensil Town

"Gristle and fat!" he cried. "Where did this girl come from?"

"I found her in the forest and brought her here a prisoner," replied the Captain.

"Why did you do that?" inquired the King, puffing his pipe lazily.

"To create some excitement," the Captain answered. "It is so quiet here that we are all getting rusty for want of amusement. For my part, I prefer to see stirring times."

"Naturally," returned the cleaver, with a nod. "I have always said, Captain, without a bit of irony, that you are a sterling officer. But what do you expect me to do with your band of prisoners?"

"That is for you to decide," declared the Captain. "You're the King."

"To be sure; to be sure," muttered the cleaver. "As you say, we have had dull times since the steel and grindstone eloped and left us. Command my Counselors and the Royal Courtiers to attend me, as well as the High Priest and the Judge. We'll then decide what can be done."

The Captain saluted and retired and Dorothy sat down on an overturned kettle and asked:

"Have you anything to eat in your kingdom?"

"Here! Get up! Get off from me!" cried a faint voice, at which his Majesty the cleaver said:

"Excuse me, but you're sitting on my friend the Tenquart Kettle."

Dorothy at once arose, and the kettle turned right side up and looked at her reproachfully.

"I'm a friend of the King, so no one dares sit on me," said he.

"I'd prefer a chair, anyway," she replied.

"Sit on that hearth," commanded the King.

So Dorothy sat on the hearth-shelf of the big range, and the subjects of Utensil Town began to gather around in a large and inquisitive throng. Toto lay at Dorothy's feet and Billina flew upon the range, which had no fire in it, and perched there as comfortably as she could.

When all the Counselors and Courtiers had assembled—and these seemed to include most of the inhabitants of the kingdom—the King rapped on the block for order and said:

"Friends and Fellow Utensils! Our worthy Commander of the Spoon Brigade, Captain Dipp, has captured the three prisoners you see before you and brought them here for—for—I don't know what for. So I ask your advice how to act in this matter, and what fate I should mete out to these captives. Judge Sifter, stand on my right. It is your business to sift through this affair. High Priest Colander, stand on my left and see that no one testifies falsely in this matter."

As these two officials took their places Dorothy asked: "Why is the colander the High Priest?"

"He's the holiest thing we have in the kingdom," replied King Kleaver. "Now, it is the duty of the King's Counselors to counsel the King at all times of emergency, so I beg you to speak out and advise me what to do with these prisoners."

"I demand that they be killed several times, until they are dead!" shouted a spice box, hopping around very excitedly.

A Visit to Utensil Town

"Compose yourself, Mr. Paprika," advised the King. "Your remarks are tangy but you need a dash of common sense. It is only necessary to kill a person once to make him dead; but I do not see that it is necessary to kill this little girl at all."

"I don't, either," said Dorothy.

"Pardon me, but you are not expected to advise me in this matter," replied King Kleaver.

"Why not?" asked Dorothy.

"You might be prejudiced in your own favor, and so mislead us," he said. "Now then, good subjects, who speaks next?"

"I'd like to smooth this thing over, in some way," said a steam iron, earnestly. "We are supposed to be useful to mankind, you know."

"But the girl isn't mankind! She's womankind!" yelled a corkscrew.

"What do you know about it?" inquired the King.

"I'm a lawyer," said the corkscrew, proudly. "I am accustomed to appearing at the bar."

"But you're crooked," retorted the King, "and that debars you. You may be a corking good lawyer, Mr. Popp, but I must ask you to withdraw your remarks."

"Very well," said the corkscrew, sadly; "I see I haven't any pull at this court."

"Permit me," continued the steam iron, "to press my suit, your Majesty. I don't wish

to gloss over any fault the prisoner may have committed, if such a fault exists; but we owe her some consideration, and that's flat!"

"I'd like to hear from Prince Karver," said the King. At this a stately carving knife stepped forward and bowed.

"The Captain was wrong to bring this girl here, and she was wrong to come," he said. "But now that the foolish deed is done let us all have a slashing good time."

"That's it! That's it!" screamed a fat chopping knife. "We'll make mincemeat of the girl and hash of the chicken and sausage of the dog!"

There was a shout of approval at this and the King had to rap again for order.

"Gentlemen, gentlemen!" he declared, "your remarks are somewhat cutting and rather disjointed, as might be expected from such acute intellects. But you give no reasons for your demands."

"See here, Kleaver, you make me tired," exclaimed a saucepan, strutting before the King very impudently. "You're about the worst King that ever reigned in Utensil Town, and that's saying a good deal. Why don't you run things yourself, instead of asking everybody's advice, like the big, clumsy idiot you are?"

The King sighed.

"I wish there wasn't a saucepan in my kingdom," he said. "You fellows are always stewing over something and every once in a while you slop over and make a mess of it. Go hang yourself, sir—by the handle—and don't let me hear from you again."

Dorothy was much shocked by the dreadful language the utensils employed; she thought that they must have had very little proper training. So she said, addressing the

A Visit to Utensil Town

King, who seemed very unfit to rule his turbulent subjects: "I wish you'd decide my fate right away. I can't stay here all day, trying to find out what you're going to do with me."

"What I'd like to know," said a can-opener, in a shrill voice, "is why the girl came to our forest, anyhow, and why she intruded upon Captain Dipp—who ought to be called Dippy—and who she is, and where she came from, and where she is going, and why and wherefore and therefore and when."

"I'm sorry to see, Sir Jabber," remarked the King to the can-opener, "that you have such a prying disposition. As a matter of fact, all the things you mention are none of our business."

"Tell me, please, what is our business?" inquired a potato-masher, winking at Dorothy somewhat impertinently. "I'm fond of little girls, myself, and it seems to me she has as much right to wander in the forest as we have."

"Who accuses the little girl, anyway?" inquired a rolling pin. "What has she done?"

"I don't know," said the King. "What has she done, Captain Dipp?"

"That's the trouble, your Majesty. She hasn't done anything," replied the Captain.

"What do you want me to do?" asked Dorothy.

This question seemed to puzzle them all. Finally a chafing dish, exclaimed, irritably: "If no one can throw any light on this subject you must excuse me if I go out."

At this a big kitchen fork pricked up its ears and said in a tiny voice: "Let's hear from Judge Sifter."

"That's proper," returned the King.

So Judge Sifter turned around slowly several times and then said, "We have nothing against the girl except the stove-hearth upon which she sits. Therefore I order her discharged."

"Discharged!" cried Dorothy. "Why, I never was discharged in my life, and I don't intend to be. If it's all the same to you, I'll resign."

"It's all the same," declared the King. "You are free—you and your companions—and may go wherever you like."

"Thank you," said the little girl. "But haven't you anything to eat in your kingdom? I'm hungry."

"Go into the woods and pick blackberries," advised the King, lying down upon his back again and preparing to take a nap. "There isn't a morsel to eat in all Utensil Town that I know of."

So Dorothy jumped up and said, "Come on, Toto and Billina. If we can't find anything to eat here, we will gather some blackberries on our way home."

The utensils drew back and allowed them to pass without protest, although Captain Dipp marched the Spoon Brigade in close order after them until they reached a fork in the road. There the spoons halted but Dorothy and her companions continued on towards the forest and home.

—*The Emerald City of Oz*, 1910

Simplicity and Kindness

In this world in which we live simplicity and kindness are the only magic wands that work wonders, and in the Land of Oz Dorothy found these same qualities had won for her the love and admiration of the people. Indeed, the little girl had made many warm friends in the fairy country, and the only real grief the Ozites had ever experienced was when Dorothy left them and returned to her Kansas home.

—*THE EMERALD CITY OF OZ*, 1910

Like Many Other Girls

Coming as she did from our world, Dorothy was much like many other girls we know; so there were many times when she was not so wise as she might have been, and other times when she was obstinate and got herself into trouble. But life in a fairyland had taught the little girl to accept all sorts of surprising things as matters-of-course, for while Dorothy was no fairy—but just as mortal as we are—she had seen more wonders than most mortals ever do.

—*THE SCARECROW OF OZ, 1915*

179

You have at least one least one magical art, Dorothy: you know the trick of winning all hearts.

—GLINDA OF OZ, 1920

DOROTHY

TOTO

The Princess looked at her more closely.

"Tell me," she resumed, "are you of royal blood?"

"Better than that, ma'am," said Dorothy. "I came from Kansas."

—OZMA OF OZ, 1907

181

A Once-in-a-While Princess

"What!" cried Polly, looking at Dorothy curiously. "Do you belong to the nobility?"

"Just in Oz I do," said the child, "because Ozma made me a Princess, you know. But when I'm home in Kansas I'm only a country girl, and have to help with the sweeping and wipe the dishes while Aunt Em washes them. Do you have to help wash dishes on the rainbow, Polly?"

"No, dear," answered Polychrome, smiling.

"Well, I don't have to work any in Oz, either," said Dorothy. "It's kind of fun to be a Princess once in a while; don't you think so?"

—*THE ROAD TO OZ, 1909*

Little Dorothy and Toto

When Dorothy and Toto tired of the grandeur of the Emerald City of Oz, they would wander out into the country and all through the land, peering into queer nooks and corners and having a good time in their own simple way. The Wizard did not approve of her traveling alone in this way, but the girl always laughed at the little man's fears for her and said she was not afraid of anything that might happen.

One day, while on such a journey, Dorothy and Toto found themselves among the wild wooded hills at the southeast of Oz—a place usually avoided by travelers because so many magical things abounded there. And, as they entered a forest path, the little girl noticed a sign tacked to a tree, which said: "Look out for Crinklink."

Toto looked at the sign so seriously that Dorothy almost believed he could read it.

"Never mind Crinklink," said she. "I don't believe anything in Oz will try to hurt us, Toto, and if I get into trouble, you must take care of me."

"Bow-wow!" said Toto, and Dorothy knew that meant a promise.

The path was narrow

and wound here and there between the trees, but they could not lose their way, because thick vines and creepers shut them in on both sides. They had walked a long time when, suddenly turning a curve of the pathway, they came upon a lake of black water, so big and so deep that they were forced to stop.

"Well, Toto," said Dorothy, looking at the lake, "we must turn back, I guess, for there is neither a bridge nor a boat to take us across the black water."

"Here's the ferryman, though," cried a tiny voice beside them, and the girl gave a start and looked down at her feet, where a man no taller than three inches sat at the edge of the path with his legs dangling over the lake.

"Oh!" said Dorothy; "I didn't see you before."

Toto growled fiercely and made his ears stand up straight, but the little man did not seem in the least afraid of the dog.

He merely repeated: "I'm the ferryman, and it's my business to carry people across the lake."

Dorothy couldn't help feeling surprised, for she could have picked the little man up with one hand, and the lake was big and broad. Looking at the ferryman more closely she saw that he had small eyes, a big nose, and a sharp chin. His hair was blue and his clothes scarlet, and Dorothy noticed that every button on his jacket was the head of some animal. The top button was a bear's head and the next button a wolf's head; the next was a cat's head and the next a weasel's head, while the last button of all was the head of a field mouse. When Dorothy looked into the eyes of these animals' heads, they all nodded and said in a chorus: "Don't believe all you hear, little girl!"

"Silence!" said the small ferryman, slapping each button head in turn, but not hard enough to hurt them. Then he

turned to Dorothy and asked: "Do you wish to cross over the lake?"

"Why, I'd like to," she answered, hesitating; "but I can't see how you will manage to carry us, without a boat."

"If you can't see, you mustn't see," he answered with a laugh. "All you need do is shut your eyes, say the word, and—over you go!"

Dorothy wanted to get across, in order that she might continue her journey. "All right," she said, closing her eyes; "I'm ready."

Instantly she was seized in a pair of strong arms so big and powerful that she was startled and cried out in fear.

"Silence!" roared a great voice, and the girl opened her eyes to find that the tiny man had suddenly grown into a giant and was holding both her and Toto in a tight embrace while in one step he spanned the lake and reached the other shore.

Dorothy became frightened, then,

especially as the giant did not stop but continued tramping in great steps over the wooded hills, crushing bushes and trees beneath his broad feet. She struggled in vain to free herself, while Toto whined and trembled beside her, for the little dog was frightened, too.

"Stop!" screamed the girl. "Let me down!" But the giant paid no attention. "Who are you, and where are you taking me?" she continued; but the giant said not a word. Close to Dorothy's ear, however, a little voice answered her, saying: "This is the terrible Crinklink, and he has you in his power."

Dorothy managed to twist her head around and found it was the second button on the jacket—the wolf's head—which had spoken to her.

"What will Crinklink do with me?" she asked anxiously.

"No one knows. You must wait and see," replied the wolf.

"Some of his captives he whips," squeaked the weasel's head.

"Some he transforms into bugs and other things," growled the bear's head.

"Some he enchants, so that they become doorknobs," sighed the cat's head.

"Some he makes his slaves—even as we are—and that is the most dreadful fate of all," added the field mouse. "As long as Crinklink exists we shall remain buttons, but as there are no more buttonholes on his jacket he will probably make you a slave."

Dorothy began to wish she had not met Crinklink. Mean-time, the giant took such big steps that he soon reached the heart of the hills, where, perched upon the highest peak, stood a log castle. Before this castle, he paused to set down Dorothy and Toto, for Crinklink was at present far too large to enter his own doorway. So he made himself grow smaller, until he was about the size of an ordinary man. Then he said to Dorothy, in stern, commanding tones: "Enter, girl!"

Dorothy obeyed and entered the castle with Toto at her heels. She found the place to be merely one big room. There was a table and chair of ordinary size near the center, and at one side a wee bed that seemed scarcely big enough for a doll. Everywhere else were dishes—dishes—dishes! They were all dirty, and were piled upon the floor, in all the corners and upon every shelf. Evidently Crinklink had not washed a dish for years, but had cast them aside as he used them.

Dorothy's captor sat down in the chair and frowned at her.

"You are young and strong, and will make a good dishwasher," said he.

"Do you mean me to wash all those dishes?" she asked, feeling both indignant and fearful, for such a task would take weeks to accomplish.

"That's just what I mean," he retorted. "I need clean dishes, for all I have are soiled, and you're going to make them clean or else. So get to work and be careful not to break anything. If you smash a dish, the penalty is one lash from my dreadful cat-o'-nine-tails for every piece the dish breaks into," and here Crinklink displayed a terrible whip that made the little girl shudder.

Dorothy knew how to wash dishes, but she remembered that often she carelessly broke one. In this case, however, a good deal depended on being careful, so she handled the dishes very cautiously.

While she worked, Toto sat by the hearth and growled low at Crinklink who

sat in his chair growling at Dorothy because she moved so slowly. He expected her to break a dish any minute, but as the hours passed away and this did not happen Crinklink began to grow sleepy. It was tiresome watching the girl wash dishes and often he glanced longingly at the tiny bed. Now he began to yawn, and he yawned and yawned until finally he said:

"I'm going to take a nap. But the buttons on my jacket will be wide awake and whenever you break a dish the crash will waken me. As I'm rather sleepy I hope you won't interrupt my nap by breaking anything for a long time."

Then Crinklink made himself grow smaller and smaller until he was three inches high and of a size to fit the tiny bed. At once he lay down and fell fast asleep.

Dorothy came close to the buttons and whispered: "Would you really warn Crinklink if I tried to escape?"

"You can't escape," growled the bear.

"Crinklink would become a giant, and soon overtake you."

"But you might kill him while he sleeps," suggested the cat, in a soft voice.

"Oh!" cried Dorothy, drawing back; "I couldn't possibly kill anything—even to save my life."

But Toto had not heard this conversation and was not so particular about killing monsters. Also the little dog knew he must try and save his mistress. In an instant he sprang upon the wee bed and was about to seize the sleeping Crinklink in his jaws when Dorothy heard a loud crash and a heap of dishes fell from the table to the floor. Then the girl saw Toto and the little man rolling on the floor together, like a fuzzy ball, and when the ball stopped rolling, there was Toto wagging his tail joyfully and there sat the little Wizard of Oz, laughing merrily at the expression of surprise on Dorothy's face.

"Yes, dear, it's me," said he, "and I've been playing tricks on you—for your own good. I wanted to prove to you that it is really dangerous for a little girl to wander alone in fairy country; so I took the form of Crinklink to teach you a lesson. There isn't any Crinklink but if there had been you'd be severely whipped for breaking all those dishes."

The Wizard now rose, took off the coat with the button heads, and spread it on the floor, wrong side up. At once there crept from beneath it a bear, a wolf, a cat, a weasel, and a field mouse, who all rushed from the room and escaped.

"Come on, Toto," said Dorothy; "let's go back to the Emerald City. You've given me a good scare, Wizard," she added, with dignity, "and perhaps I'll forgive you; but just now I'm mad to think how easily you fooled me."

—*LITTLE WIZARD STORIES*, 1914

A Lot of Nightmare

Children love a lot of nightmare and at least a little heartache written into their books. And they get them in the Oz books. I know that I went through excruciatingly lovely nightmares and heartaches when the Scarecrow lost its straw, when the Tin Woodman was taken apart, when the Saw-horse broke his wooden leg (it hurt me, even if it didn't Mr. Baum).

—JAMES THURBER,
THE NEW REPUBLIC,
DECEMBER 12, 1934

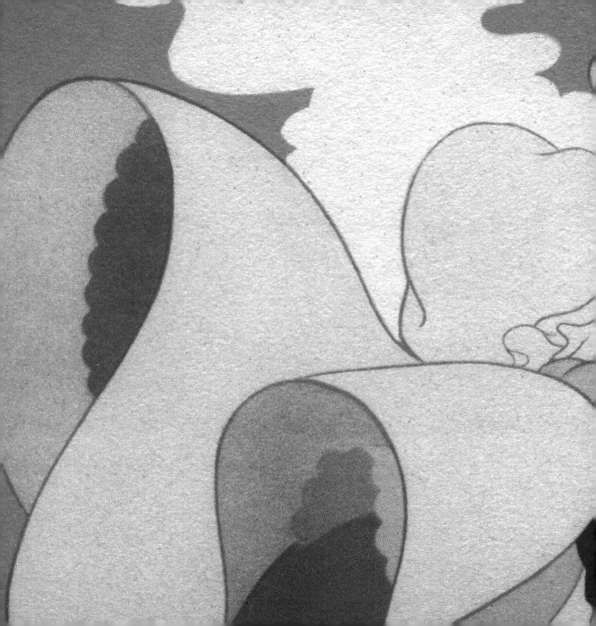

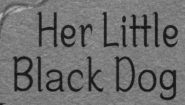

Her Little Black Dog

It was Toto who made Dorothy laugh, and saved her from growing as gray as her other surroundings. Toto was not gray; he was a little black dog, with long, silky hair and small black eyes that twinkled merrily on either side of his funny, wee nose. Toto played all day long, and Dorothy played with him and loved him dearly.

—THE WONDERFUL
WIZARD OF OZ,
1900

Toto's Secret

That's my dog Toto," said Dorothy, "and he's the kindest dog in all the world. Toto knows a good many things, too; almost as much as I do, I guess. He can't talk, not being a fairy dog. He's just a common United States dog; but that's a good deal; and I understand him, and he understands me, just as well as if he could talk."

—*THE PATCHWORK GIRL OF OZ*, 1913

Without Toto, Dorothy would never have discovered the way home. Her rush to save him from the storm initiates her journey to Oz. Later, chasing Toto rather than accepting the balloon ride home protects her from becoming caught forever in the Wizard's illusion of power. It is Toto who discovers the humbug hiding behind a screen, and Toto prevents Dorothy from flying off in his repaired balloon. Well-intentioned witches and wizards must not interfere with Dorothy. She must find the means within for saving herself. The impetus and guidance for her success in Oz is sparked by her devotion to Toto and her strong instinctive responses to life's circumstances.

—GITA DOROTHY MORENA, GREAT-GRANDDAUGHTER OF L. FRANK BAUM, *THE WISDOM OF OZ*, 1998

Do all the animals in Oz talk?" Betsy asked Dorothy and Ozma. "Almost all," answered Dorothy. "There's a Yellow Hen here, and she can talk, and so can her chickens; and there's a Pink Kitten upstairs in my room who talks very nicely; but I've a little fuzzy black dog, named Toto, who has been with me in Oz a long time, and he's never said a single word but 'Bow-wow!'"

A KANSAS DOG

"Do you know why?" asked Ozma.

"Why, he's a Kansas dog; so I suppose he's different from these fairy animals," replied Dorothy. "Hank the Donkey isn't a fairy animal, any more than Toto," said Ozma, "yet as soon as he came under the spell of our fairyland he found he could talk. It was the same way with Billina, the Yellow Hen whom you brought here at one time. The same spell has affected Toto, I assure you; but he's a wise little dog and while he knows everything that is said to him he prefers not to talk."

"Goodness me!" exclaimed Dorothy. "I never suspected Toto was fooling me all this time." Then she drew a small silver whistle from her pocket and blew a shrill note upon it.

A KANSAS DOG

A moment later there was a sound of scurrying footsteps, and a shaggy black dog came running up the path.

Dorothy knelt down before him and shaking her finger just above his nose she said:

"Toto, haven't I always been good to you?"

Toto looked up at her with his bright black eyes and wagged his tail.

"Bow-wow!" he said, and Betsy knew at once that meant yes, as well as Dorothy and Ozma knew it, for there was no mistaking the tone of Toto's voice.

"That's a dog answer," said Dorothy. "How would you like it, Toto, if I said nothing to you but 'bow-wow?'"

Toto's tail was wagging furiously now, but otherwise he was silent.

"Really, Dorothy," said Betsy, "he can talk with his bark and his tail just as well as we can. Don't you understand such dog language?"

A KANSAS DOG

"Of course I do," replied Dorothy. "But Toto's got to be more sociable. See here, sir!" she continued, addressing the dog, "I've just learned, for the first time, that you can say words . . . if you want to. Don't you want to, Toto?"

"Woof!" said Toto, and that meant "no."

"Not just one word, Toto, to prove you're as good as any other animal in Oz?"

"Woof!"

"Just one word, Toto . . . and then you may run away." He looked at her steadily a moment. "All right. Here I go!" he said, and darted away as swift as an arrow.

Dorothy clapped her hands in delight, while Betsy and Ozma both laughed heartily at her pleasure and the success of her experiment.

—TIK-TOK OF OZ, 1914

Marching to the Song of Johnny Dooit

The only way to do a thing
Is do it when you can,
And do it cheerfully, and sing
And work and think and plan.
The only real unhappy one
Is he who dares to shirk;
The only really happy one
Is he who cares to work.

—THE ROAD TO OZ, 1909

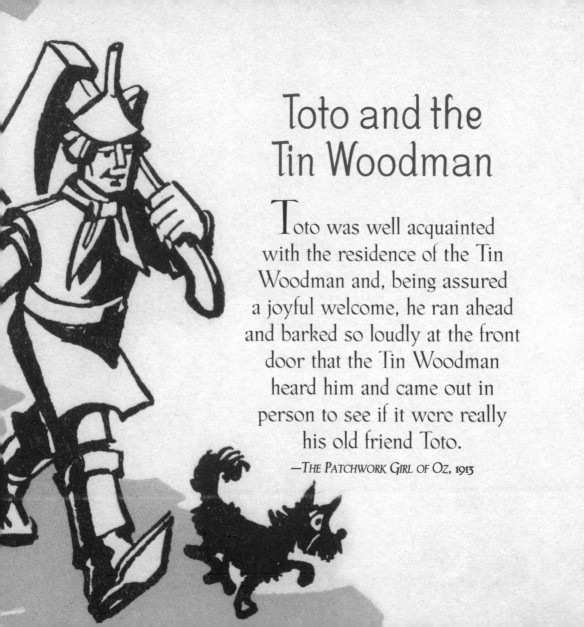

Toto and the Tin Woodman

Toto was well acquainted with the residence of the Tin Woodman and, being assured a joyful welcome, he ran ahead and barked so loudly at the front door that the Tin Woodman heard him and came out in person to see if it were really his old friend Toto.

—THE PATCHWORK GIRL OF OZ, 1913

What Toto Lost

Toto and his friends were peacefully enjoying the end of a busy day when the dog made a startling announcement. "I've lost my growl!" said the little dog. "What do you suppose has become of it?"

"If you'd asked me to keep track of your growl, I might be able to tell you," remarked the Lion sleepily. "But, frankly, Toto, I supposed you were taking care of it yourself."

"It's an awful thing to lose one's growl," said Toto, wagging his tail sadly. "What if you lost your roar, Lion? Wouldn't you feel terrible?"

"My roar," replied the Lion, "is the fiercest thing about me. I depend on it to frighten my enemies so badly that they won't dare to fight me."

"Once," said the Mule, "I lost my bray, so that I couldn't call to Betsy to let her know I was hungry. It was certainly very uncomfortable not to be able to make a noise."

"You make enough noise now," declared Toto. "But none of you has answered my question: Where is my growl?"

"You may search me," said the Woozy. "I don't care for such things myself."

"No, but you snore terribly," asserted Toto.

"What one does when asleep one is not accountable for," said the Woozy. "I wish you would wake me up, some time when I'm snoring, and let me hear the sound. Then I can judge whether it is terrible or delightful."

"It isn't pleasant, I assure you," said the Lion, yawning.

"You ought to break yourself of the habit," said the Sawhorse. "You never hear me snore, because I never sleep. I don't even whinny, as those puffy meat horses do. I wish that whoever stole Toto's growl had taken the Mule's bray and the Lion's roar and the Woozy's snore at the same time."

"Do you think, then, that my growl was stolen?"

"You have never lost it before, have you?" inquired the Sawhorse.

"Only once, when I had a sore throat from barking too long at the moon."

"Is your throat sore now?" asked the Woozy.

"No," replied the dog.

"I can't understand," said Hank, "why dogs bark at the moon. They can't scare the moon, and the moon doesn't pay any attention to the bark. So why do dogs do it?"

"Were you ever a dog?" asked Toto.

"No, indeed," replied Hank. "I am thankful to say I was created a mule—the most beautiful of all beasts—and have always remained one."

What Toto Lost

The Woozy sat upon his square haunches to examine Hank with care.

"Beauty," he said, "must be a matter of taste. I don't say your judgment is bad, friend Hank, or that you are so vulgar as to be conceited. But if you admire big waggly ears, and a tail like a paint-brush, and hoofs big enough for an elephant, and a long neck and a body so skinny that one can count the ribs with one eye shut—if that's your idea of beauty, Hank—then either you or I must be much mistaken."

"You're full of edges," sneered the Mule. "If I were square, as you are, I suppose you'd think me lovely."

"Outwardly, dear Hank, I would," replied the Woozy. "But to be really lovely one must be beautiful without and within."

The Lion, regarding the two calmly with his great yellow eyes, said to the dog:

"My dear Toto, our friends have taught us a lesson in humility. If the Woozy and the Mule are indeed as beautiful as they seem to think, you and I must be ugly."

"Not to ourselves," protested Toto. "I am a fine dog and you are a fine lion. Only in comparison with one another can we be properly judged, so I will leave it to the Sawhorse to decide which is the most beautiful animal among us all. The Sawhorse is wood, so he won't be prejudiced and will speak the truth."

"I surely will," responded the Sawhorse. "Are you all agreed to accept my judgment?"

"We are!" they declared, each one hopeful.

"Then," said the Sawhorse, "I must point out to you the fact that you are all meat creatures, who tire unless they sleep, and starve unless they eat, and suffer from thirst unless they drink. Such animals must be very imperfect, and imperfect creatures cannot be beautiful. Now, I am made of wood and, if you wish my honest judgment, I will confess that among us all I am the most beautiful."

The Mule snorted and the Woozy laughed; Toto had lost his growl and could only look scornfully at the Sawhorse. But the Lion stretched himself and yawned, saying quietly:

"Were we all like the Sawhorse we would all be Sawhorses, which would be too many of the kind; were we all like Hank, we would be a herd of mules; if like Toto, we would be a pack of dogs; should we all become the shape of the Woozy, he would no longer be remarkable for his unusual appearance. Finally, were you all like me, I would consider you so common that I would not care to associate with you. To be individual, my friends, to be different from others, is the only way to become distinguished from the common herd. Let us be glad, therefore, that we differ from one another in form and in disposition."

"There is some truth in that speech," remarked Toto. "But how about my lost growl?"

"The growl is of importance only to you," responded the Lion, "so it is your business to worry over the loss, not ours. If you love us, do not inflict your burdens on us; be unhappy all by yourself."

"If someone stole my growl," said the little dog, "I hope we shall find him very soon and punish him as he deserves. He must be the most cruel person in all the world, for to prevent a dog from growling when it is his nature to growl is just as wicked, in my opinion, as stealing all the magic in Oz."

"Why would anyone steal your growl?" asked the Lion.

What Toto Lost

"Well," said the dog, "it was a wonderful growl, soft and low and—and—"

"And ragged at the edges," said the Sawhorse.

"See here," said the Lion, "this chatter is keeping us all awake and tomorrow is likely to be a busy day. Go to sleep and forget your quarrels."

"Friend Lion," retorted the dog, "if I hadn't lost my growl you would hear it now."

The Lion sighed. "If only you had lost your voice, when you lost your growl," said he, "you would be a more agreeable companion."

But they quieted down, after that, and soon the entire camp was wrapped in slumber. Toto still worried over his lost growl, but like a wise little dog kept his worry to himself.

A few days later, Toto awoke to make a happy discovery that he ran to share with his friends. "I've found my growl at last!" said Toto, standing before the Lion and wagging his tail.

"Let's hear," said the Lion.

"Gr-r-r-r-r!" said Toto.

"That's a very respectable growl for a small dog. Where did you find it, Toto?"

"I was smelling in the corner by the pantry," said Toto, "when suddenly a mouse ran out—and I growled!"

"Just like that? Well, then you made a great fuss over nothing, didn't you?" remarked the Woozy.

And Toto growled at him. Long and happily.

—*THE LOST PRINCESS OF OZ*, 1917

215

In Joyous Greeting

Toto barked at the Cowardly Lion in joyous greeting, for he knew the beast of old and loved him, and it was funny to see how gently the Lion raised his huge paw to pat Toto's head.

—THE ROAD TO OZ, 1909

The Cowardly Lion Gets the Evil Eye

It was a rare treat for Uncle Henry and Aunt Em, who had lived in Kansas all their lives and known little enjoyment of any sort, to move to the Emerald City. They got to wear beautiful clothes and live in a palace and be treated with respect and consideration by all around them. They were very happy indeed as they strolled up the shady walks and looked upon the gorgeous flowers and shrubs, feeling that their new home was more beautiful than any tongue could describe.

Suddenly, as they turned a corner and walked through a gap in a high hedge, they came face to face with an enormous Lion, which crouched upon the green lawn and seemed surprised by their appearance.

They stopped short, Uncle Henry trembling with horror and Aunt Em too terrified to scream. "If I only had a gun—" said Uncle Henry.

"Haven't you, Henry? Haven't you?" she asked anxiously.

"No gun, Em. So let's die as brave and graceful as we can."

"I won't die. I won't be eaten by a lion!" wailed Aunt Em, glaring upon the huge beast. Then a thought struck her, and she whispered: "Henry, I've heard that savage beasts can be conquered by the human eye. I'll stare that lion down and save our lives."

"Try it, Em," he returned, also in a whisper. "Look at him as you look at me when I'm late for dinner."

Aunt Em turned upon the Lion with a determined and wild eye. She glared at the immense beast steadily, and the Lion, who had been quietly blinking at them, began to appear uneasy and disturbed.

"Is anything the matter, ma'am?" he asked, in a mild voice.

His speech startled Aunt Em and Uncle Henry. "Hold on, Em!" Uncle Henry exclaimed. "Quit the eagle eye conquest and take courage. This must be the same Cowardly Lion Dorothy has told us about."

"Oh?" she asked, much relieved, regarding the animal with new interest. "Are you the Cowardly Lion?" she inquired. "Are you Dorothy's friend?"

"Yes'm," answered the Lion, meekly. "Dorothy and I are old pals and are very fond of each other. I'm the King of Beasts, you know, and the Hungry Tiger and I serve Princess Ozma as her body guards."

"To be sure," said Aunt Em, nodding. "But the King of Beasts shouldn't be cowardly."

"I've heard that said before," remarked the Lion, "but that does not keep me from being frightened whenever I go into battle."

"What do you do, run?" asked Uncle Henry.

"No; that would be foolish, for the enemy would run after me," declared the Lion. "So I tremble with fear and pitch in as hard as I can; and so far I have always won my fight."

The Cowardly Lion Gets the Evil Eye

"Were you scared when I looked at you just now?" inquired Aunt Em.

"Terribly scared, madam," answered the Lion, "for at first I thought you were going to have a fit. Then I noticed you were trying to overcome me by the power of your eye, and your glance was so fierce and penetrating that I shook with fear."

This greatly pleased the lady, and she said quite cheerfully, "Well, I won't hurt you, so don't be scared any more. I just wanted to see what the human eye was good for."

"The human eye is a fearful weapon," remarked the Lion, scratching his nose softly with his paw to hide a smile. "Had I not known you were Dorothy's friends I might have torn you both into shreds in order to escape your terrible gaze."

Aunt Em shuddered at hearing this, and Uncle Henry said hastily, "I'm glad you knew us. Good morning, Mr. Lion; we'll hope to see you again, some time in the future."

"Good morning," replied the Lion, squatting down upon the lawn again. "You are likely to see a good deal of me, if you live in the Land of Oz."

—*THE EMERALD CITY OF OZ*, 1910

King of Beasts

All the other animals in the forest naturally expect me to be brave, for the Lion is everywhere thought to be the King of Beasts. I learned that if I roared very loudly every living thing was frightened and got out of my way. Whenever I've met a man I've been awfully scared; but I just roared at him, and he has always run away as fast as he could go. If the elephants and the tigers and the bears had ever tried to fight me, I should have run myself—I'm such a coward; but just as soon as they hear me roar they all try to get away from me, and of course I let them go."

—**The Cowardly Lion**, THE WONDERFUL WIZARD OF OZ, 1900

222

The Wizard of Ice

This season brought the twenty-first annual edition of the Ice Capades to New York City. Its feature number was a thirteen-minute production of *The Wizard of Oz*. The star was Lynne "Patsy" Finnegan who, as Dorothy, carried a small, fluffy-haired poodle under her arm. After she released the Scarecrow from his pole in the cornfield, he danced and sang, "If I Only Had a Brain" followed by a chorus of six scarecrows, identically dressed. When they encountered the Tin Woodman and the Cowardly Lion, each of those characters was joined by a similarly dressed chorus.

Upon arrival in the Emerald City, a curtain parted revealing a huge mechanical head resting on a pillow. After Dorothy denounced it as a "humbug," the Wizard himself came skating out from behind the head and proceeded to grant the travelers' wishes. Dorothy was sent back to Kansas by balloon.

—AS REVIEWED IN *THE BAUM BUGLE*, FEBRUARY 1966

And when she tired,
Dot would ride
Atop the Lion's
thickset hide.
—INGE U. LOSTDAMSEL,
THE WIZARD OF OZ,
A LIMERICK VERSION, 1984

Why He Isn't a Coward

I'm not afraid to go anywhere, if the Cowardly Lion is with me. I know him pretty well, and so I can trust him. He's always afraid, when we get into trouble, and that's why he's cowardly; but he's a terrible fighter, and that's why he isn't a coward. He doesn't like to fight, you know, but when he has to, there isn't any beast living that can conquer him."

—**Dorothy**, THE MAGIC OF OZ, 1919

An Ozzy Thing About England

The pubs, a venerable English institution, specialize in ale and beer, and most of them are licensed to carry only one brand of beer. Different brands predominate in different regions of Britain, and the brand sold by a particular pub is named in large letters on a colorful sign outside the establishment. In the region between London and Oxford the most common brand is called "Courage," so on the road to London one encounters pub after pub with signs outside them displaying simply the word "Courage," and inside, presumably, Englishmen sit sipping courage—much as the Cowardly Lion once did. Now the oddest thing about this is that on a recent trip to Cardiff in Wales we found that a great many of the Cardiff pubs sold (exclusively) a local brand of beer called "Brains."

I'm now looking around for a brand called "Heart."

—C. Warren Hollister, *The Best of the Baum Bugle*, 1965–1966

My head is quite empty but once I had brains, and a heart also; so, having tried them both, I should much rather have a heart.

—**Tin Woodman,** *THE WONDERFUL WIZARD OF OZ*, 1900

The Value of Love

The Tin Woodman is a startling reminder of the value of love. It is ironical that this fictional character made of metal harbors such a burning desire for a heart. Although he appears stiff and rigid, in the nurturing presence of a loving woman, he is free to express the compassion and tenderness that reside within his armor of metal. The Tin Woodman encourages us to respect our feelings of love and tenderness, and honor the importance of heartfelt connection.

—GITA DOROTHY MORENA, GREAT-GRANDDAUGHTER OF L. FRANK BAUM, *THE WISDOM OF OZ*, 1998

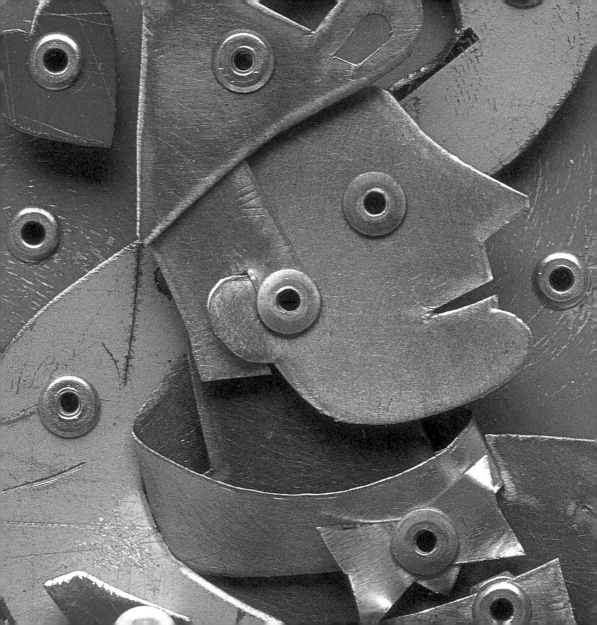

Oz never
did give
nothing
to the
Tin Man that
he didn't
already have.

—"Tin Man," America, 1974

At Home with the Tin Woodman

The Tin Woodman is one of the most important creatures in all Oz. Emperor of the Winkies, he is a personal friend of Ozma, to whom he owes allegiance. Known as something of a dandy, he keeps his tin body brilliantly polished and his tin joints well oiled. Also he is very courteous in manner and so kind and gentle that everyone loves him dearly....

Tin is plentiful in the Winkie Country and the Winkies are said to be the most skillful tinsmiths in the world. So the Tin Woodman hired them to build his magnificent castle, which is all of tin, from the ground to the tallest turret, and so brightly polished that it glitters in the sun's rays more gorgeously than silver.

In the handsome tin parlor, all the floors are made of tin. The walls are paneled with tin and from the tin ceilings hang tin chandeliers. Every bit of furniture—tables, beds, desks, couches—is made of brightly polished tin.

Around the grounds of the castle is a tin wall, with tin gates; but the gates are left standing wide open because the Emperor has no enemies to disturb him. There are tin trees, too, with tin benches and swings to sit upon. Also, on the sides of the pathway leading up to the front door of the castle, are rows of tin statues, very cleverly executed, of Dorothy, Toto, the Scarecrow, the Wizard, the Shaggy Man, Jack Pumpkinhead and Ozma, all standing upon neat pedestals of tin.

Visitors to the Tin Castle are greeted warmly by the Tin Woodman of Oz. "It gives me great pleasure to entertain you in my castle," he tells his guests, "there is room enough to spare. And if anyone wishes to be nickel-plated, my valet will do it free of charge." ∾○⌢

—*THE PATCHWORK GIRL OF OZ*, 1913

T
is the Tin

that they
make
into toys,

that walk by
themselves

and puzzle
small boys.

—POEM BY W. W. DENSLOW,
DENSLOW'S ABC BOOK, 1903

The Scarecrow and the Tin Woodman

One morning the Tin Woodman went to visit his friend the Scarecrow, and as they had nothing better to do they decided to take a boat ride on the river. So they got into the Scarecrow's boat, which was formed from a big corncob, hollowed out and pointed at both ends and decorated around the edges with brilliant jewels. The sail was of purple silk and glittered in the sunshine.

There was a good breeze that day, so the boat glided swiftly over the water. Soon they came to a smaller river that flowed from out a deep forest and the Tin Wood man proposed they sail up this stream, as it would be cool and shady beneath the trees of the forest. So the Scarecrow, who was steering, turned the boat up the stream and the friends continued talking together of old times and the wonderful adventures they had met with while traveling with Dorothy, the little Kansas girl. They became so interested in this talk that they forgot to notice that the boat was now sailing through the forest or that the stream was growing more narrow and crooked.

Suddenly the Scarecrow glanced up and saw a big rock just ahead of them. "Look out!" he cried; but the warning came too late.

The Tin Woodman sprang to his foot just as the boat bumped into the rock, and the jar made him lose his balance. He toppled and fell overboard and being made of tin he sank to the bottom of the water in an instant and lay there at full length, face up.

Immediately the Scarecrow threw out the anchor, so as to hold the boat in that place, and then he leaned over the side and through the clear water looked at his friend sorrowfully. "Dear me!" he exclaimed; "what a misfortune!"

"It is, indeed," replied the Tin Woodman, speaking in muffled tones because so much water covered him. "I cannot drown, of course, but I must lie here until you find a way to get me out. Meantime, the water is soaking into all my joints and I shall become badly rusted before I am rescued."

"Very true," agreed the Scarecrow; "but be patient, my friend, and I'll dive down and get you. My straw will not rust, and is easily replaced, if damaged, so I'm not afraid of the water."

The Scarecrow now took off his hat and made a dive from the boat into the water; but he was so light in weight that he barely dented the surface of the stream, nor could he reach the Tin Woodman with his outstretched straw arms. So he floated to the boat and climbed into it, saying the while: "Do not despair, my friend. We have an extra anchor aboard, and I will tie it around my waist, to make me sink, and dive again."

"Don't do that!" called the Tin Man. "That would anchor you also to the bottom, where I am, and we'd both be helpless."

"True enough," sighed the Scarecrow, wiping his wet face with a handkerchief; and then he gave a cry of astonishment, for he found he had wiped off one painted eye and now had but one eye to see with.

"How dreadful!" said the poor Scarecrow. "That eye must have been painted in watercolor, instead of oil. I must be

careful not to wipe off the other eye, for then I could not see to help you at all."

A shriek of elfish laughter greeted this speech and looking up the Scarecrow found the trees full of black crows, who seemed amused by the straw man's one-eyed countenance. He knew the crows well, however, and they had usually been friendly to him because he had never deceived them into thinking he was a meat man—the sort of man they really feared. "Don't laugh," said he; "you may lose an eye yourselves some day."

"We couldn't look as funny as you, if we did," replied one old crow, the king of them. "But what has gone wrong with you?"

"The Tin Woodman, my dear friend and companion, has fallen overboard and is now on the bottom of the river," said the Scarecrow. "I'm trying to get him out again, but I fear I won't succeed."

"Why, it's easy enough," declared the old crow. "Tie a string to him and all of my crows will fly down, take hold of the string, and pull him up out of the water. There are hundreds of us here, so our united strength could lift much more than that."

"But I can't tie a string to him," replied the Scarecrow. "My straw is so light that I am unable to dive through the water. I've tried it, and knocked one eye out."

"Can't you fish for him?"

"Ah, that is a good idea," said the Scarecrow. "I'll make the attempt."

He found a fish line in the boat, with a stout hook at the end of it. No bait was needed, so the Scarecrow dropped the hook into the water till it touched the Woodman.

"Hook it into a joint," advised the crow, who was now perched upon a branch that stuck far out and bent down over the water.

The Scarecrow tried to do this, but having only one eye he could not see the joints very clearly.

"Hurry up, please," begged the Tin Woodman; "you've no idea how damp it is down here."

"Can't you help?" asked the crow.

"How?" inquired the Tin Man.

"Catch the line and hook it around your neck."

The Tin Woodman made the attempt and after several trials wound the line around his neck and hooked it securely.

"Good!" cried the King Crow, a mischievous old fellow. "Now, then, we'll all grab the line and pull you out."

At once the air was filled with black crows, each of whom seized the cord with beak or talons. The Scarecrow watched them with much interest and forgot that he had tied the other end of the line around his own waist, so he would not lose it while fishing for his friend.

"All together for the good caws!" shrieked the King Crow, and with a great flapping of wings the birds rose into the air.

The Scarecrow clapped his stuffed hands in glee as he saw his friend drawn from the water into the air; but the next moment the straw man was himself in the air, his stuffed legs kicking wildly; for the crows had flown straight up through the trees. On one end of the line dangled the Tin Woodman, hung by the neck, and on the other dangled the Scarecrow, hung by the waist and clinging fast to the spare anchor of the boat, which he had seized hoping to save himself.

"Hey, there—be careful!" shouted the Scarecrow to the crows. "Don't take us so high. Land us on the river bank."

But the crows were bent on mischief. They thought it a good joke to bother the two, now that they held them captive.

"Here's where the crows scare the Scarecrow!" chuckled the naughty King Crow, and at his command the birds flew over the forest to where a tall dead tree stood higher than all the other trees. At the very top was a crotch, formed by two dead limbs, and into the crotch the crows dropped the center of the line. Then, letting go their hold, they flew away, chattering with laughter, and left the two friends suspended high in the air—one on each side of the tree.

Now the Tin Woodman was much heavier than the Scarecrow, but the reason they balanced so nicely was because the straw man still clung fast to the iron anchor. There they hung, not ten feet apart, yet unable to reach the bare tree-trunk.

"For goodness sake don't drop that anchor," said the Tin Woodman anxiously.

"Why not?" inquired the Scarecrow.

"If you did I'd tumble to the ground, where my tin would be badly dented by the fall. Also you would shoot into the air and land somewhere among the tree-tops."

"Then," said the Scarecrow, earnestly, "I will hold on to the anchor!"

For a time they both dangled in silence, the breeze swaying them gently to and fro. Finally the Tin Woodman said: "Here is an emergency, friend, where only brains can help us. We must think of some way to escape."

"I'll do the thinking," replied the Scarecrow. "My brains are the sharpest."

He thought so long that the Tin Woodman grew tired and tried to change his position, but found his joints had already rusted so badly that he could not move them. And his oilcan was back in the boat. "Do you suppose your brains are rusted, friend Scarecrow?" he asked in a weak voice, for his jaws would scarcely move.

"No, indeed. Ahh, here's an idea at last!"

And with this the Scarecrow clapped his hands to his head, forgetting the anchor, which tumbled to the ground. The result was astonishing; for, just as the Tin Man had said, the light Scarecrow flew into the air, sailed over the top of the tree and landed in a bramble-bush, while the Tin Man fell to the ground, and landing on a bed of dry leaves was not dented at all. The Tin Woodman's joints were so rusted, however, that he was unable to move, while the thorns held the Scarecrow a fast prisoner.

While they were in this sad plight the sound of hoofs was heard and along the forest path rode the little Wizard of Oz, seated on a wooden Sawhorse. He smiled when he saw the one-eyed head of the Scarecrow sticking out of the bramble-bush, but he helped the poor straw man out of his prison.

"Thank you, dear Wiz," said the grateful Scarecrow. "Now we must get the oilcan and rescue the Tin Woodman."

Together they ran to the river bank, but the boat was floating in midstream and the Wizard was obliged to mumble some magic words to draw it to the bank, so the Scarecrow could get the oilcan. Then back they ran to the Tin Woodman, and while the Scarecrow carefully oiled each joint the little Wizard moved the joints gently back and forth until they worked freely. After an hour of this labor the Tin Woodman was again on his feet, and although still a little stiff he managed to walk to the boat.

The Wizard and the Sawhorse also got aboard the corncob craft and together they returned to the Scarecrow's palace. But the Tin Woodman was very careful not to stand up in the boat again.

—*LITTLE WIZARD STORIES, 1914*

We are the hollow men
We are the stuffed men

— T. S. ELIOT, FROM "THE HOLLOW MEN," 1925

We Are Not Built the Same

I believe it's magic and that someone is playing a trick on us . . ."

"Then let us shut our eyes and walk forward," suggested the Tin Woodman.

"Excuse me," replied the Scarecrow. "My eyes are not painted to shut. Because you happen to have tin eyelids, you must not imagine we are all built in the same way."

—*THE MARVELOUS LAND OF OZ*, 1904

Imagination

Imagination has brought mankind through the Dark Ages to its present state of civilization. Imagination led Columbus to discover America. Imagination led Franklin to discover electricity. Imagination has given us the steam engine, the telephone, the talking-machine and the automobile; for these things had to be dreamed of before they became realities. So I believe that dreams—day dreams, you know, with your eyes wide open and your brain-machinery whizzing—are likely to lead to the betterment of the world. The imaginative child will become the imaginative man or woman most apt to create, to invent, and therefore to foster civilization. A prominent educator tells me that fairy tales are of untold value in developing imagination in the young. I believe it.

—L. FRANK BAUM, PREFACE, *THE LOST PRINCESS OF OZ*, 1917

252

The Land of the Munchkins
is full of surprises.
—THE TIN WOODMAN OF OZ, 1918

Safe in the funny little
    Munchkins town
The tired cyclone dropped
    her down,
Where the Witch of the North
    gave her Silver Shoes
Which the Witch of the East
    was too dead to use. →

She started then for the
    Emerald City
When a winking Scarecrow
    claimed her pity.

From his lonely pole she
    lifted him down
And he joined in the walk
    to Emerald town.

—Souvenir cookie box issued in
conjunction with the 1903 stage
production of *The Wizard of Oz* in
which the character of Toto was
replaced by a cow named Imogene

256

Czech, 1962

France, 1960

Dorothy Meets the Scarecrow

he Wizard of Oz is perhaps the most frequently reprinted and translated American children's story ever published. Virtually every illustrated edition of the book includes the scene where Dorothy meets the Scarecrow.

W. W. Denslow was the first artist to show us these characters and he set the gold standard for all the others to follow. Every artist who ever drew this scene created their own personal vision of Oz and of these two seminal characters. Here are alternate artistic interpretations from around the world.

Poland, 1983

U.S., 1950

U.S., 1899

Bulgaria, 1978

Israel, 1988

Italy, 1961

Italy, 1944

Scarecrow Affirmations

Nothing can resist a kind heart and a sharp axe.

—*THE MARVELOUS LAND OF OZ*, 1904

Experience has taught me that I can do anything
if I but take time to think it out.

—*THE MARVELOUS LAND OF OZ*, 1904

If the thing can be accomplished at all,
it is in a very simple manner.

—*THE MARVELOUS LAND OF OZ*, 1904

The only people worthy of consideration
are the unusual ones.

—*THE MARVELOUS LAND OF OZ*, 1904

Everything in life is unusual until
you get accustomed to it.

—*THE MARVELOUS LAND OF OZ*, 1904

Near to Quarreling

"If you wish to meet with real cleverness," remarked the Scarecrow, "you should visit the Munchkin farmer who first made *me*. I won't say that my friend the Emperor isn't all right for a tin man, but any judge of beauty can understand that a Scarecrow is far more artistic and refined."

"You are too soft and flimsy," said the Tin Woodman.

"You are too hard and stiff," said the Scarecrow, and this was as near to quarreling as the two friends ever came.

—*The Tin Woodman of Oz*, 1918

The Scarecrow's Lament

Though I appear a handsome man,
I'm really stuffed with straw;
It's difficult, a man to plan,
Without a single flaw.

Though you may think my lovely head
A store of love contains,
The farmer made this lovely frame
And quite forgot my brains.

When brains are lacking in a head,
It's usually the rule,
That wisdom from the man has fled,
And he remains a fool.

So though my charms are very great,
As I am well assured,
I'll never reach my full estate
Till brains I have secured.

—LYRICS WRITTEN BY L. FRANK BAUM FOR THE 1903
STAGE PRODUCTION OF *THE WIZARD OF OZ*

Don't Call Me a Fool

Y ou see," the Scarecrow continued, confidentially, "I don't mind my legs and arms and body being stuffed, because I cannot get hurt. If anyone treads on my toes or sticks pins into me, it doesn't matter, for I can't feel it. But I do not want people to call me a fool, and if my head stays stuffed with straw instead of with brains, as yours is, how am I ever to know anything?"

—*THE WONDERFUL WIZARD OF OZ, 1900*

269

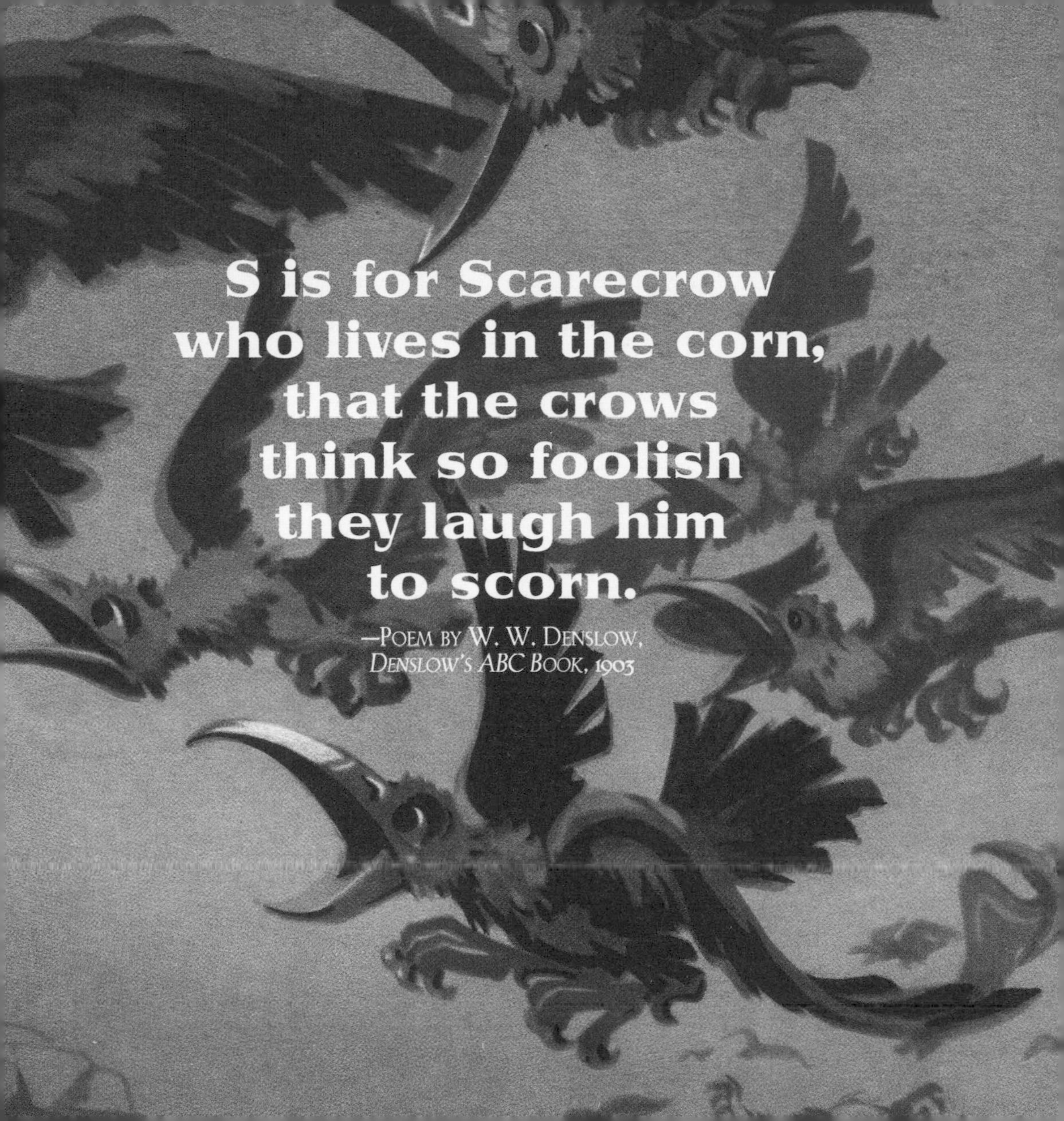

S is for Scarecrow
who lives in the corn,
that the crows
think so foolish
they laugh him
to scorn.

—POEM BY W. W. DENSLOW,
DENSLOW'S ABC BOOK, 1903

All Wrong, Somehow

There was no reply. So the boy called to the King: "Are you all right, your majesty?"

The Scarecrow groaned.

"I'm all wrong, somehow," he said in a weak voice.

—*THE MARVELOUS LAND OF OZ*, 1904

The Scarecrow's house is shaped like an immense ear of corn. The rows of kernels are made of solid gold, and the green upon which the ear stands upright is a mass of sparkling emeralds. Perched upon the very top of the structure is a figure representing the Scarecrow himself. You can imagine how big this ear of corn is when I report that a single gold kernel forms a window, swinging outward upon hinges, while a row of four kernels opens to make the front entrance. Inside there are five stories, each story being a single room. The lower room is a grand reception hall. The walls are hung with white silk, upon which flocks of black crows are embroidered in black diamonds. Some of the chairs are made in the shape of big crows and upholstered with cushions of corn-colored silk. The second story contains a fine banquet room, where the Scarecrow entertains his guests, and the three stories above that are bedrooms exquisitely furnished and decorated.

"From these rooms," said the Scarecrow, proudly, "are fine views of the surrounding cornfields. The corn I grow is always husky, and I call the ears my regiments, because they have so many kernels. Of course I cannot ride my cobs, but I really don't care shucks about that. Taken altogether, my farm stacks up with any in the neighborhood."

—*THE EMERALD CITY OF OZ*, 1910

AT HOME
WITH THE
SCARECROW

My Father, L. Frank Baum

My father wrote all of his books in longhand on a clipboard containing single sheets of white typewriter paper and a great deal of his writing was done in his garden, which he loved and cherished. He would make himself comfortable in a garden chair, cross his legs, place the clipboard on one knee, and with a cigar in his mouth, begin writing whenever the spirit moved him. This is the picture I have of him in my mind which I most frequently recall. When he finished an episode or adventure, he would get up and work in the garden. He might putter around for two or three hours before returning to his writing; or it might be two or three days or a week before the idea he was seeking came to him. "My characters just won't do what I want them to," he would explain. He rarely made a wrong move and did little revision; the few longhand manuscript pages which survive are remarkably clean copy. He then went up to a reconverted bedroom that acted as his study. After a book was completed, Father typed it himself, using the first

two fingers of each hand and developing a good speed. It was during this typing that he made any changes or revisions that seemed necessary.

—HARRY NEAL BAUM, L. FRANK BAUM'S SON,
THE AMERICAN BOOK COLLECTOR, DECEMBER 1962

There are worse things in the world than being a Scarecrow.

—THE WONDERFUL WIZARD
OF OZ, 1900

The last end of a wait, however long

it has been, is the hardest to endure.

—THE TIN WOODMAN OF OZ, 1918

We Could Talk About Oz for Hours

When I visit the Conways, I often talk to Big Eustace about *The Wizard of Oz* books, the wonderful series of fantasy stories that L. Frank Baum wrote back at the turn of the century. It seems that Big Eustace and I were both raised reading the same beautiful hardcover editions of these books. (In Mr. Conway's childhood, he received one book a year as a Christmas present, while I inherited the entire antique set from my grandmother.) Most people don't know that there were sequels to the original Dorothy Gale story, so Big Eustace was delighted to find that I knew the stories well and could recall each lush Art Deco illustration and discuss the most obscure characters. Tik-Tok, Billina the Chicken, the Hungry Tiger, the Gnome King, the Rollers, and Polychrome (the rainbow's daughter)—and I know them all, and so does he, and we can talk about that stuff for hours.

—ELIZABETH GILBERT, *THE LAST AMERICAN MAN*, 2002

281

The Wisdom of Oz

Nothing is gained by haste. Careful thought may aid us, and so may the course of events. The unexpected is always likely to happen, and cheerful patience is better than reckless action.

—**Ozma**, *GLINDA OF OZ*, 1920

Perhaps it is better to be a machine that does its duty than a flesh-and-blood person who will not, for a dead truth is better than a live falsehood.

—*THE ROAD TO OZ*, 1909

Contentment with one's lot is true wisdom.

—**Yip**, *THE LOST PRINCESS OF OZ*, 1917

Fear does not make one a coward but I believe it is more easy to avoid danger than to overcome it. The safest way is the best way, even for one who is brave and determined.

—**Woot**, *THE TIN WOODMAN OF OZ*, 1918

If you think of some dreadful thing, it's liable to happen, but if you don't think of it, and no one else thinks of it, it just *can't* happen.

—**Scarecrow**, *THE TIN WOODMAN OF OZ*, 1918

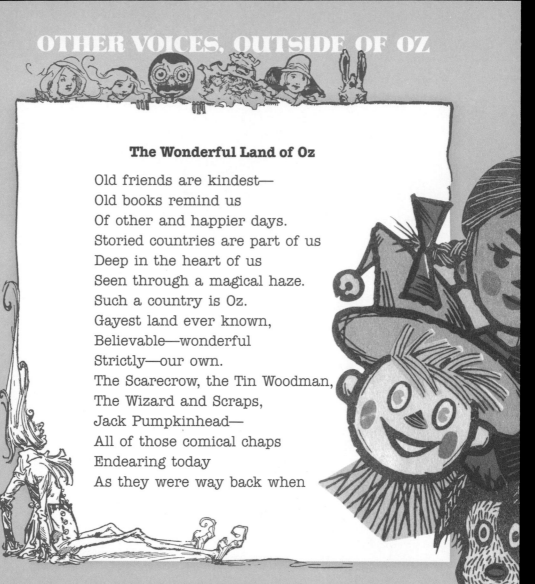

The Wonderful Land of Oz

Old friends are kindest—
Old books remind us
Of other and happier days.
Storied countries are part of us
Deep in the heart of us
Seen through a magical haze.
Such a country is Oz.
Gayest land ever known,
Believable—wonderful
Strictly—our own.
The Scarecrow, the Tin Woodman,
The Wizard and Scraps,
Jack Pumpkinhead—
All of those comical chaps
Endearing today
As they were way back when

We ourselves were a blithe
And adventurous ten!
And, with thousands I know,
Though I speak for myself,
The Oz books rank first
On fond memories shelf.

—RUTH PLUMLY THOMPSON,
PUBLISHED IN *THE BAUM BUGLE*

Editor's Note: Thompson wrote 19 Oz books in
the series following the death of L. Frank Baum.

In a fairy country such as
ours every undiscovered
place is likely to harbor
wicked creatures.

—THE LOST PRINCESS OF OZ, 1917

Этhis evil creature is old and ugly. She lost one eye many years ago and wears a black patch over it, so the people of Jinxland named her "Blinkie." Of course witches are forbidden to exist in the Land of Oz, but Jinxland is far removed from the center of Ozma's dominions, and so totally cut off from it by the steep mountains and the bottomless gulf, that the laws of Oz are not obeyed very well in that country.

BLINKIE

Consequently, there are several witches in Jinxland who are the terror of the people, but King Krewl favors them and permits them to exercise their evil sorcery. Blinkie is the leader of all the other witches and therefore the most hated and feared. The King uses her witchcraft at times to assist him in carrying out his cruelties and revenge, but he has to pay Blinkie large sums of money or heaps of precious jewels before she even considers undertaking an enchantment for him. This makes the King hate the old woman almost as much as his subjects do.

—*THE SCARECROW OF OZ*, 1915

This is always the way with wicked people. They cannot be trusted even by one another.

—THE MAGIC OF OZ, 1919

Dorothy Was Innocent

"Y ou are welcome, most noble Sorceress, to the land of the Munchkins. We are so grateful to you for having killed the Wicked Witch of the East, and for setting our people free from bondage."

Dorothy listened to this speech with wonder. What could the little woman possibly mean by calling her a sorceress, and saying she had killed the Wicked Witch of the East? Dorothy was an innocent, harmless little girl, who had been carried by a cyclone many miles from home; and she had never killed anything in all her life.

—*THE WONDERFUL WIZARD OF OZ*, 1900

Now the Wicked Witch has a great longing to have for her own the Silver Shoes which the girl always wore. Her Bees and her Crows and her Wolves were lying in heaps and drying up, and she had used up all the power of the Golden Cap; but if she could only get hold of the Silver Shoes they would give her more power than all the other things she had lost. She watched Dorothy carefully, to see if she ever took off her shoes, thinking she might steal them.

But the child was so proud of her pretty shoes that she never took them off except at night and when she took her bath.

HER PRETTY SHOES

—*THE WONDERFUL WIZARD OF OZ*, 1900

I will give you my kiss, and no one will dare injure a person who has been kissed by the Witch of the North.

—**Glinda**, *THE WONDERFUL WIZARD OF OZ*, 1900

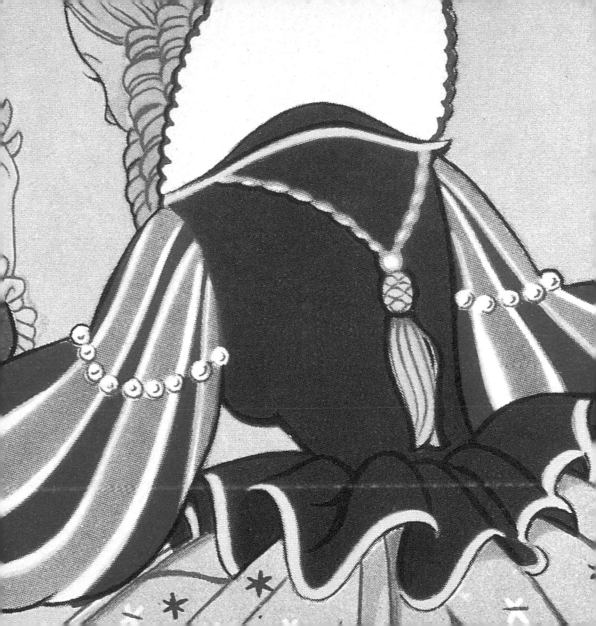

The Witch Did Not Bleed

Now the Wicked Witch of the West had but one eye, yet that was as powerful as a telescope, and could see everywhere . . .

Dorothy and Toto could find no way out of the castle, for it was constantly guarded by the yellow Winkies, who were the slaves of the Wicked Witch and too afraid of her not to do as she told them.

Dorothy had to work hard during the day, and often the Witch threatened to beat her with the same old umbrella she always carried in her hand. But, in truth, she did not dare strike Dorothy, because of the mark upon her forehead. The child did not know this and was full of fear for herself and Toto. Once the Witch struck Toto a blow with her umbrella and the brave little dog flew at her and bit her leg in return. The Witch did not bleed where she was bitten, for she was so wicked that the blood in her had dried up many years before.

—THE WONDERFUL WIZARD OF OZ, 1900

Is Dorothy Guilty of Murder?

Several elementary schools have recently put Dorothy on trial for killing the Wicked Witch of the West. According to "Junior Barristers Square Off over Dorothy's Deadly Deed" (*Orange County Register*, June 5th, 1992), the girl was judged in class by a jury of her peers—fourth-, fifth-, and sixth-graders. It is a clever way of teaching students the fundamentals of the American judicial system. Dorothy usually gets off. But she really should learn how to control her temper!

—Michael Patrick Hearn,
The Annotated Wizard
of Oz, 2000

Wizard's Words of Wisdom

All you need is confidence in yourself.
—*The Wonderful Wizard of Oz*, 1900

There is no living thing that is not afraid when it faces danger.
—*The Wonderful Wizard of Oz*, 1900

True courage is in facing danger when you are afraid.
—*The Wonderful Wizard of Oz*, 1900

Experience is the only thing that brings knowledge, and the longer you are on earth, the more experience you are sure to get.
—*The Wonderful Wizard of Oz*, 1900

Foolish fears, and worries over nothing, with a mixture of nerves and ifs, will soon make a Flutterbudget of any one.
—*The Emerald City of Oz*, 1910

No one
can do more
than his best.
—*THE MAGIC OF OZ*, 1919

I think you are a very bad man," said Dorothy.
"Oh no, my dear; I'm really a very good man; but I'm a very bad Wizard I must admit."
—THE WONDERFUL WIZARD OF OZ, 1900

What They Wanted from Him

W hy do you wish to see the terrible Oz?" asked the man.

"I want him to give me some brains," said the Scarecrow, eagerly.

"Oh, Oz could do that easily enough," declared the man. "He has more brains than he needs."

"And I want him to give me a heart," said the Tin Woodman.

"That will not trouble him," continued the man, "for Oz has a large collection of hearts, of all sizes and shapes."

"And I want him to give me courage," said the Cowardly Lion.

"Oz keeps a great pot of courage in his throne room," said the man, "which he has covered with a golden plate, to keep it from running over. He will be glad to give you some."

"And I want him to send me back to Kansas," said Dorothy.

"Where is Kansas?" asked the man, in surprise.

"I don't know," replied Dorothy, sorrowfully; "but it is my home, and I'm sure it's somewhere."

—*The Wonderful Wizard of Oz*, 1900

305

A Bag of Magic

From the books of Oz ancestors we know that
the Wizard of Oz, who lives in Ozma's palace,
has been taught much powerful magic by Glinda
and has a bag of magic tools
which he brought with him
from Kansas.

—*THE LOST PRINCESS OF OZ*, 1917

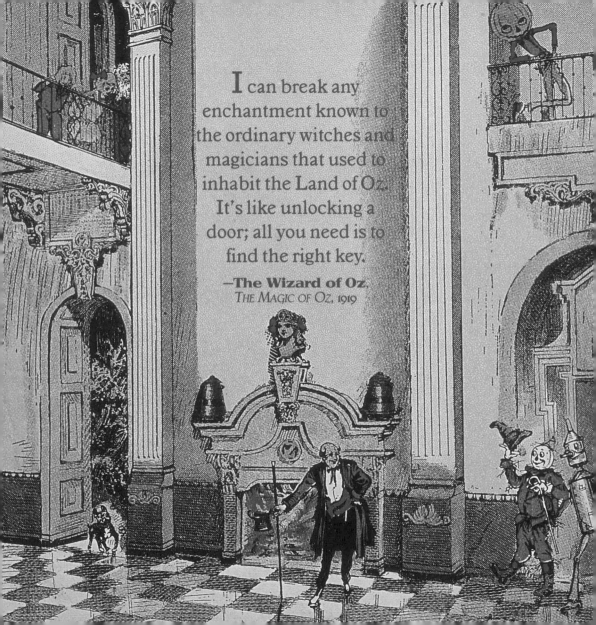

I can break any enchantment known to the ordinary witches and magicians that used to inhabit the Land of Oz. It's like unlocking a door; all you need is to find the right key.

—The Wizard of Oz,
THE MAGIC OF OZ, 1919

The Autobiography of the Wonderful Wizard of Oz

I was born in Omaha, and my father, who was a politician, named me Oscar Zoroaster Phadrig Isaac Norman Henkle Emmannuel Ambroise Diggs, Diggs being the last name because he could think of no more to go before it. Taken altogether, it was a dreadfully long name to weigh down a poor innocent child, and one of the hardest lessons I ever learned was to remember my own name. When I grew up I just called myself O. Z., because the other initials were P-I-N-H-E-A-D; and that spelled 'pinhead,' which was a reflection on my intelligence.

"When a young man I ran away from home and joined a circus. I used to call myself a Wizard, and do tricks of ventriloquism."

"What does that mean?" asked the Princess.

"Throwing my voice into any object I pleased, to make it appear that the object was speaking instead of me. Also I began to make balloon ascensions. On my balloon and on all the other articles I used in the circus I painted the two initials: 'O. Z.', to show that those things belonged to me.

"One day my balloon ran away with me and brought me across the deserts to this beautiful country. When the people saw me come from the sky they naturally thought me some superior creature, and bowed down before me. I told them I was a Wizard, and showed them some easy tricks that amazed them; and when they saw the initials painted on the balloon they called me Oz.

"At that time, there were four separate countries in this Land, each one of the four being ruled by a Witch. But the people thought my power was greater than that of the Witches: and perhaps the Witches thought so too, for they never dared oppose me. I ordered the Emerald City to be built just where the four countries cornered together, and when it was completed I announced myself the Ruler of the Land of Oz, which included all the four countries of the Munchkins, the Gillikins, the Winkies and the Quadlings. Over this Land I ruled in peace for many years, until I grew old and longed to see my native city once again. So when Dorothy was first blown to this place by a cyclone I arranged to go away with her in a balloon; but the balloon escaped too soon and carried me back alone. After many adventures I reached Omaha, only to find that all my old friends were dead or had moved away. So, having nothing else to do, I joined a circus again, and made my balloon ascensions until the earthquake caught me and returned me to Oz and here I shall remain till the end of my days."

—DOROTHY AND THE WIZARD IN OZ, 1908

Never So Wonderful

T he Wonderful Wizard was never so wonderful as Queen Ozma," the people said to one another, in whispers; "for he claimed to do many things he could not do; whereas our new Queen does many things no one would ever expect her to accomplish."

—*THE MARVELOUS LAND OF OZ, 1904*

Confessions of the Wizard of Oz

One of my greatest fears was the Witches, for while I had no magical powers at all I soon found out that the Witches were really able to do wonderful things. There were four of them in this country, and they ruled the people who live in the North and South and East and West. Fortunately, the Witches of the North and South were good, and I knew they would do me no harm; but the Witches of the East and West were terribly wicked and had they not thought I was more powerful than themselves, they would surely have destroyed me. As it was, I lived in deadly fear of them for many years; so you can imagine how pleased I was when I heard that your house had fallen on the Wicked Witch of the East. When you came to me, Dorothy, I was willing to promise anything if you would only do away with the other Witch; but, now that you have melted her, I am ashamed to say that I cannot keep my promises.

—**The Wizard of Oz**, THE WONDERFUL WIZARD OF OZ, 1900

He's only a humbug Wizard, though," said Dorothy.

"And that is the safest kind of a Wizard to have," replied Ozma, promptly.

—Dorothy and the Wizard in Oz, 1908

To become self-reliant, you must trust your own inner nature and love yourself. Then, if the Wizard tells you to bring back the broomstick of the Wicked Witch of the West, you will pay absolutely no attention to that man behind the curtain.

—JOEY GREEN, *THE ZEN OF OZ: TEN SPIRITUAL LESSONS FROM OVER THE RAINBOW*, 1998

The Fuddles Fall Apart

While traveling to Fuddlecumjig to meet the Fuddles, Dorothy and her friends met a kangaroo who joined them on their journey. They had traveled a short distance when, by and by the Wizard paused to ask, "Are the Fuddles nice people?"

"Oh, very nice," answered the kangaroo; "that is, when they're properly put together. But they get dreadfully scattered and mixed up, at times, and then you can't do anything with them."

"What do you mean by their getting scattered?" inquired Dorothy.

"Why, they're made in a good many small pieces," explained the kangaroo; "and whenever any stranger comes near them they have a habit of falling apart and scattering themselves around. That's when they get so dreadfully mixed, and it's a hard puzzle to put them together again."

"Who usually puts them together?" asked Omby Amby.

"Any one who is able to match the pieces. I've put them together a good many times myself because every time I come near they scatter themselves."

"I should think they would get used to your coming, and not be afraid," said Dorothy.

"It isn't that," replied the kangaroo. "They're not a bit afraid when they're put together and usually they're very jolly and pleasant. It's just a habit they have, to scatter themselves, and if they didn't do it they wouldn't be Fuddles."

"I don't see much use our visiting these Fuddles," remarked Aunt Em. "If we find them scattered, all we can do is to sweep them up, and then go about our business."

"Oh, I believe we'd better go on," replied Dorothy. "I'm getting hungry, and we must try to get some luncheon at Fuddlecumjig. Perhaps the food won't be scattered as badly as the people."

"You'll find plenty to eat there," declared the kangaroo, hopping along in big bounds; "and they have a fine cook, too, if you can manage to put him together. There's the town now—just ahead of us!"

They looked ahead and saw a group of very pretty houses standing in a green field a little apart from the main road.

"Some Munchkins came here a few days ago and matched a lot of people together," said the kangaroo. "I think they are together yet, and if you go softly, without making any noise, perhaps they won't scatter."

"Let's try it," suggested the Wizard.

So after bidding good-bye to the kangaroo, who hopped away home, they entered the field and very cautiously approached the group of houses.

So silently did they move that soon they saw through the windows of the houses, people moving around. They seemed much like other people, from a distance, and apparently they did not notice the little party so quietly approaching.

They had almost reached the nearest house when Toto saw a large beetle crossing

The Fuddles Fall Apart

the path and barked loudly at it. Instantly a wild clatter was heard from the houses and yards. Dorothy thought it sounded like a sudden hailstorm, and the visitors, knowing that caution was no longer necessary, hurried forward to see what had happened.

After the clatter an intense stillness reigned in the town. The strangers entered the first house they came to, which was also the largest, and found the floor strewn with pieces of the people who lived there. They looked much like fragments of wood neatly painted, and were of all sorts of curious and fantastic shapes, no two pieces being in any way alike.

They picked up some of these pieces and looked at them carefully. Dorothy held one piece which was an eye and looked at her pleasantly but with an interested expression, as if it wondered what she was going to do with it. Quite nearby she discovered and picked up a nose and by matching the two pieces together found that they were part of a face.

"If I could find the mouth," she said, "this Fuddle might be able to talk, and tell us what to do next."

"Then let us find it," replied the Wizard, and so all got down on their hands and knees and began examining the scattered pieces.

The Fuddles Fall Apart

"I've found it!" cried the Shaggy Man, and ran to Dorothy with a queer-shaped piece that had a mouth on it. But when they tried to fit it to the eye and nose they found the parts wouldn't match together.

"That mouth belongs to some other person," said Dorothy. "You see we need a curve here and a point there, to make it fit the face."

"Well, it must be here some place," declared the Wizard; "so if we search long enough we shall find it."

Dorothy fitted an ear on next, and the ear had a little patch of red hair above it. So while the others were searching for the mouth she hunted for pieces with red hair, and found several of them which, when matched to the other pieces, formed the top of a man's head. She had also found the other eye and the ear by the time Omby Amby in a far corner discovered the mouth. When the face was thus completed all the parts joined together with a nicety that was astonishing.

"Why, it's like a picture puzzle!" exclaimed the little girl. "Let's find the rest of him, and get him all together."

"What's the rest of him like?" asked the Wizard. "Here are some pieces of blue legs and green arms, but I don't know whether they are his or not."

"Look for a white shirt and a white apron," said the head which had been put together, speaking in a rather faint voice. "I'm the cook."

"Oh, thank you," said Dorothy. "It's lucky we started you first, for I'm hungry and you can be cooking something for us to eat while we match the other folks together."

It was not so very difficult, now that they had a hint as to how the man was dressed,

to find the other pieces belonging to him, and as all of them now worked on the cook, trying piece after piece to see if it would fit, they finally had the cook set up complete.

When he was finished he made them a low bow and said, "I will go at once to the kitchen and prepare your dinner. You will find it something of a job to get all the Fuddles together, so I advise you to begin on the Lord High Chigglewitz, whose first name is Larry. He's a bald-headed, fat man and is dressed in a blue coat with brass buttons, a pink vest and drab breeches. A piece of his left knee is missing, having been lost years ago when he scattered himself too carelessly. That makes him limp a little, but he gets along very well with half a knee. As he is the chief personage in this town of Fuddlecumjig, he will be able to welcome you and assist you with the others. So it will be best to work on him while I'm getting your dinner."

"We will," said the Wizard, "and thank you very much, Cook, for the suggestion."

Aunt Em was the first to discover a piece of the Lord High Chigglewitz. "It seems to me like a fool business, this matching folks together," she remarked; "but as we haven't anything to do till dinner's ready we may as well get rid of some of this rubbish. Here, Henry, get busy and look for Larry's bald head. I've got his pink vest, all right."

They worked with eager interest, and Billina proved a great help to them. The Yellow Hen had sharp eyes and could put her head close to the various pieces that lay scattered around. She would examine the Lord High Chigglewitz and see which piece of him was next needed, and then hunt around until she found it. So before an hour had passed old Larry was standing complete before them.

"I congratulate you, my friends," he said, speaking in a cheerful voice. "You are certainly the cleverest people who ever visited us. I was never matched together so quickly in my life. I'm considered a great puzzle, usually."

"Well," said Dorothy, "there used to be a picture puzzle craze in Kansas, and so I've had some experience matching puzzles. But the pictures were flat, while you are round, and that makes you harder to figure out."

"Thank you, my dear," replied old Larry, greatly pleased. "I feel highly complimented. Were I not a really good puzzle there would be no object in my scattering myself."

"Why do you do it?" asked Aunt Em, severely. "Why don't you behave yourself, and stay put together?"

The Lord High Chigglewitz seemed annoyed by this speech; but he replied, politely: "Madam, you have perhaps noticed that every person has some peculiarity. Mine is to scatter myself. What your own peculiarity is I will not venture to say; but I shall never find fault with you, whatever you do."

Uncle Henry laughed, "This is a queer country, Em, and we may as well take people as we find them."

"If we did, we'd leave these folks scattered," she returned, and this retort made everybody laugh good-naturedly.

Then the cook came to call them to dinner, and they found an inviting meal prepared for them. The Lord High Chigglewitz sat at the head of the table and the guests had a merry time and thoroughly enjoyed themselves.

The Fuddles Fall Apart

After dinner they went out into the yard and matched several other people together, and this work was so interesting that they might have spent the entire day at Fuddlecumjig had not the Wizard suggested that they resume their journey.

"But I don't like to leave all these poor people scattered," said Dorothy, undecided what to do.

"Oh, don't mind us, my dear," returned old Larry.

"Every day or so some of the Gillikins, or Munchkins, or Winkies come here to amuse themselves by matching us together, so there will be no harm in leaving these pieces where they are for a time. But I hope you will visit us again, and if you do you will always be welcome, I assure you."

"Don't you ever match each other?" she inquired.

"Never; for we are no puzzles to ourselves, and so there wouldn't be any fun in it."

They now said good-bye to the queer Fuddles and got into their wagon to continue their journey.

"Those are certainly strange people," remarked Aunt Em, thoughtfully, as they drove away from Fuddlecumjig, "but I really can't see what use they are, at all."

"Why, they amused us all for several hours," replied the Wizard. "That is being of use to us, I'm sure."

"I think they're more fun than playing solitaire," declared Uncle Henry, soberly. "For my part, I'm glad we visited the Fuddles."

—*THE EMERALD CITY OF OZ,* 1910

Higgledy, piggledy, dee—
What fools magicians be!
His head's so thick
He can't think quick,
So he takes advice from me.

—*THE PATCHWORK GIRL OF OZ*, 1913

333

LOVE AT FIRST SIGHT

Allow me, Miss Patchwork," said the Shaggy Man, "to present my friend, the Right Royal Scarecrow of Oz. Scarecrow, this is Miss Scraps Patches; Scraps, this is the Scarecrow. Scarecrow— Scraps; Scraps—Scarecrow."

They both bowed with much dignity.

"Forgive me for staring so rudely," said the Scarecrow, "but you are the most beautiful sight my eyes have ever beheld."

"That is a high compliment from one who is so beautiful himself," murmured Scraps, casting down her suspender-button eyes by lowering her head. "But, tell me, good sir, are you not a trifle lumpy?"

"Yes, of course; that's my straw, you know. It bunches up, sometimes, in spite of all my efforts to keep it even. Doesn't your straw ever bunch?"

"Oh, I'm stuffed with cotton," said Scraps. "It never bunches, but it's inclined to pack down and make me sag."

"But cotton is a high-grade stuffing. I may say it is even more stylish, not to say aristocratic, than straw," said the Scarecrow politely. "Still, it is but proper that one so entrancingly lovely should have the best stuffing there is going. I—er—I'm so glad I've met you, Miss Scraps! Introduce us again, Shaggy."

"Once is enough," replied the Shaggy Man, laughing at his friend's enthusiasm.

—*THE PATCHWORK GIRL OF OZ*, 1913

Love Has Nine Lives

I can do lots of clever magic, but love is a stubborn thing to conquer. When you think you've killed it, it's liable to bob up again as strong as ever. I believe love and cats have nine lives.

—**Blinkie**, *The Scarecrow of Oz*, 1915

I "WITCH" YOU WOULD BE MY VALENTINE

BE MINE!

Come with me down the yellow brick road

and be my VALENTINE

Theme Song for
"Tales of the Wizard of Oz"

They're three sad souls, oh me, oh my
No brains, no heart, he's much too shy
But never mind, you three
Here's the Wizard as you can see
He'll fix that one, two, three

In the funny place called the World of Oz

Oh, the World of Oz is a very funny place
Where everyone wears a funny, funny face
All the streets are paved with gold
And no one ever grows old

On that funny land lives the Wizard of Oz

—THE RANKIN & BASS CARTOON SERIES "TALES OF THE WIZARD OF OZ" RAN FROM 1961 TO 1963

How Many People Have Read *The Wizard of Oz*?

The book sold five million copies by the time it went into the public domain in 1956, the year of its author's centenary. No one has dared estimate how many more millions have been sold since. It has been estimated that the 1939 musical based on Baum's story has been seen by more people more times than any other movie ever made. It is probably the most widely quoted film in Hollywood history (usually lines not written by L. Frank Baum).

When the Children's Literature Association took a poll of its members in 1976 to determine the most important American children's books of the last two hundred years, *The Wizard of Oz* easily made the top ten. Its fame has not been limited to the country in which it was written. *The Wizard of Oz* today is probably the most frequently translated American children's book.

—MICHAEL PATRICK HEARN, *THE ANNOTATED WIZARD OF OZ*, 2000

OTHER VOICES, OUTSIDE OF OZ

That Pot of Gold Is a Home

The simple, homespun philosophy of *The Wizard of Oz* is there is no place like home, that everybody has a heart, a brain, courage, and these are the gifts that are given to you when you come on this earth. Use them properly and you will reach the pot of gold at the end of the rainbow and that pot of gold is a home. Oz shows us that a home is not just a house, an abode, material things; it's the people who live there, the ones you love, the ones who love you that are a home.

—RAY BOLGER, FROM HIS
INTRODUCTION TO A 1978 EDITION
OF *THE WIZARD OF OZ*

Oigan las canciones,
"Sobre el Arco Iris"
"Ding! dong!, la bruja ha muerto"
"El alegre país de Oz"
y otras, cantadas por *Judy Garland*

JUDY GARLAND · FRANK MORGAN

RAY BOLGER · BERT LAHR · JACK HALEY · BILLIE BURKE

DIRECTOR: Victor Fleming

Metro Goldwyn Mayer

EL MAGO DE

En TECNICOLOR

Earth is a
beautiful place!

—**Trot**, *THE SCARECROW
OF OZ*, 1915

Further Reading

Reality and unreality are so intertwined that it is often difficult to know where one leaves off and the other begins.

—L. FRANK BAUM, "WHY THE WIZARD OF OZ KEEPS ON SELLING,"
THE ANNOTATED WIZARD OF OZ, 2000

OZ BOOKS WRITTEN BY L. FRANK BAUM

The Wonderful Wizard of Oz (also published as *The Wizard of Oz*), 1900
Illustrated by W.W. Denslow

The Marvelous Land of Oz (also published as *The Land of Oz*), 1904
Illustrated by John R. Neill

Ozma of Oz, 1907
Illustrated by John R. Neill

Dorothy and the Wizard of Oz, 1908
Illustrated by John R. Neill

The Road to Oz, 1909
Illustrated by John R. Neill

The Emerald City of Oz, 1910
Illustrated by John R. Neill

The Patchwork Girl of Oz, 1913
Illustrated by John R. Neill

Little Wizard Stories of Oz, 1913
Illustrated by John R. Neill

Tik-Tok of Oz, 1914
Illustrated by John R. Neill

The Scarecrow of Oz, 1915
Illustrated by John R. Neill

Rinkitink in Oz, 1916
Illustrated by John R. Neill

The Lost Princess of Oz, 1917
Illustrated by John R. Neill

The Tin Woodman of Oz, 1918
Illustrated by John R. Neill

The Magic of Oz, 1919
Illustrated by John R. Neill

Glinda of Oz, 1920
Illustrated by John R. Neill

The International Wizard of Oz Club

The International Wizard of Oz Club welcomes fans, collectors and scholars who just can't seem to get enough of L. Frank Baum and Oz. Founded in 1957 by a thirteen-year-old boy, the Oz Club has published *The Baum Bugle* three times a year ever since. Today, its members hold annual conventions in different areas of the country, maintain Club archives in the heart of San Francisco, and work—on a volunteer basis—to keep rare Oz material in print.

The *Bugle* includes biographical, historical, and critical studies about Oz and its creators. It shares collectors' checklists and commentary about the people and places within Oz. The *Bugle* regularly features articles on Oz in the movies and on stage, reviews new editions of books about Oz or the talented people associated with it, and reports current Oz news. Rare photographs and drawings illustrate the journal, which usually features full-color covers.

In addition to *The Baum Bugle*, the Club reprints rare titles as well as original Oz books, maps of Oz, and fun short stories by its members. One Club title, *Bibliographia Oziana* is a respected resource for collectors and dealers; it provides detailed descriptions for first and early editions of the Oz books. Collectors also appreciate fund-raising auctions held by the not-for-profit group at its regional conventions.

The Club's website, www.OzClub.org, offers everything from discussion forums and ordering information to a chronological history of Oz. Links connect the Club to many privately hosted Oz sites sponsored by IWOC members.

For more about all things Oz, readers are invited to visit the website or write:

The International Wizard of Oz Club
1407 A Street, Suite D
Antioch, California 94509

About the Art

This book includes art from various editions of *The Wizard of Oz* and the sequels that followed. By country, these artists include:

American

W. W. Denslow: illustrated L. Frank Baum's *Father Goose: His Book* in 1899, *The Wonderful Wizard of Oz* in 1900 and *Dot and Tot in Merryland* in 1901. Then he and Baum had a falling out which ended their collaboration. Denslow published his own collection of short stories using some of the characters from Oz.

Denslow, *The Wonderful Wizard of Oz*: 4 (the original copyright page), 6–7, 9, 10–11, 65, 66, 68, 120, 157, 178, 193, 196, 202, 214 (center), 222, 236–237, 248–249 (original title page), 259, 304, 305, 326.

Scarecrow and the Tin Man and Other Stories: 37, 50, 51, 88–89, 96, 129, 134, 227, 262, 264–265, 278–279.

John R. Neill: illustrated thirty-five Oz books, a group of small volumes known as "Little Wizard Stories" and wrote three of the later sequels in the Oz series. This book includes illustrations from all the Oz books penned by Baum and five that were written by Ruth Plumly Thompson after Baum's death: Endpapers, 1, 7 (right), 8, 26, 30, 31, 41, 42, 44, 45, 46, 49, 55, 58–59, 62, 76, 79, 81, 83, 85 (right), 90–91, 93, 94, 97 (top), 98 (left), 99, 100–111, 113, 118, 122–123, 124, 127, 128, 133, 141 (right), 146-147, 164, 166, 171, 172, 175, 176, 180, 182, 183, 184, 185, 187, 188–189, 191, 192, 195, 206, 210, 218, 223, 226, 229, 235, 238–247, 252, 263, 267, 272–273, 275, 276–277, 288, 289, 306, 307, 308, 309, 310, 311, 312–313, 316–317, 320, 328, 332–333, 334–335, 336–337.

38-39, 301: Evelyn Copelman, *The Wizard of Oz*, Bobbs Merrill Co., 1944.

98 (top), 157, 292: Al Hirschfeld, promotional stationery for the MGM movie, 1939.

53, 252–253: Oskar Lebeck, *The Wizard of Oz*, Grosset & Dunlap, 1939.

74–75, 233, 268: Julian Wehr, *The Wizard of Oz*, Saalfield Publishers, 1944.

Argentinean

203, 293: Freixas, *El Mago de Oz* (*The Wizard of Oz*), 1960.

Bengali

340: Dust jacket from a 1960s edition of *The Wizard of Oz*.

British

28–29, 136–137, 158–159: Hand-tinted still from the MGM movie, used to illustrate the 1940 Hutchinson & Co. edition of *The Wizard of Oz*.

151: Cover from the 1940 Hutchinson & Co. edition of *The Land of Oz Storybook*.

Hungarian

145, 298: Zsoldos Vera Rajzaibol, *The Wizard of Oz*, Budapest, 1966.

Italian

2–3, 286–287, 299, 300, 319: Raviola, *Il Mago di Oz*, 1971.

19, 97 (bottom), 255, 296–297: Miki Ferro Pelizzari, *Ozma Regina di Oz* (*Ozma of Oz*), 1944.

20–21, 126, 198-199, 205, 314: Miki Ferro Pelizzari, *Nel Rigno di Oz* (*The Kingdom of Oz*), 1944.

32–33: Carla Ruffinelli, cover for *Il Mago di Oz*, comic book adaptation of the MGM movie.

43, 169, 177 (right): Carla Ruffinelli, *Oz in Pericolo* (*The Emerald City of Oz*), 1947.

5, 253, 295: Miki Ferro Pelizzari, *Oz Paese Incantato* (*The Land of Oz*), 1947.

Japanese
138–139: 1970s edition of *The Wizard of Oz*.

Latvian
114–115, 154, 208–209, 270–271, 285: Oskar Muiznieks, *The Wizard of Oz*, 1962.

Polish
52, 60, 150, 254 (background): Zbigniew Rychlicki, *The Wizard of Oz*, 1980.

Portuguese
35, 63, 257 (inset), 302, 315: Hugo Manuel, *O Feiticeiro de Oz* (*The Wizard of Oz*), 1940.

Rumanian
200, 216–217: Wolny Alexandru, *The Wizard of Oz*, 1965.

Russian
72–73: Cover of a Russian board game for *The Wizard of the Emerald City*, 1990.

98 (center), 144, 152–153, 177 (bottom), 197, 202 (bottom), 215, 221, 230, 269, 282–283: L. Vladimirskov, *The Wizard of Oz*, which was published in Russian as *The Wizard of the Emerald City*, 1960.

155, 290–291, 294: *The Wizard of the Emerald City*, 2000.

179: L. Vladimirskov, postcard set based on *Urfin Jus and His Wooden Soldiers*, a sequel to *The Wizard of Oz* by Alexander Volkov, 1963.

Uzbek
284 (center): *The Wizard of Oz*, 1966.

318: Dust jacket, *The Wizard of Oz*, 1966.

Other images in the book are from the following sources:

10: Portrait of Willard Carroll in the Oz room of his home in the Hollywood Hills by Richard Glenn.

11: Stationery featuring the Oz characters, 1925.

14–15: Promotional map, Henry Regnery Company, 1968.

16–17: Hungarian LP record album, interior spread, 1980.

18: Border design from a title card of the silent movie, *The Patchwork Girl of Oz*, 1914.

22–23: Cover of a board game based on *Tales of the Wizard of Oz* cartoon series, Lowell Manufacturers, 1961.

24: Still from the silent film, *The Wizard of Oz*, directed by and starring (as the Scarecrow) Larry Semon, 1925.

34: Dick Martin's dust jacket design for *Glinda of Oz*, 1960.

About the Art

47: *Tales of the Wizard of Oz* scarecrow doll, 1961.

48: Ken Barr illustration for *Tik-Tok of Oz Coloring and Activity Book*, unpublished tie-in to *Return to Oz*, 1985.

49: "Hangers from The Merrie Land of Oz," manufactured by Barney Stempler & Sons, with drawings featuring characters from the MGM movie, 1940s.

54: Background illustration from the animated cartoon series, *Off to See the Wizard*, 1967. Inset: Newspaper photo of Margaret Hambleton from a clipping reporting on the premiere of the Junior League production of *The Land of Oz*, Chicago, 1928.

56: Paint by Numbers illustration from the Craftint Company, 1950.

57 (background): The unpainted version of the Paint by Numbers set is much rarer. Inset: Handmade bronze sculpture of the Tin Man character, 1970s.

61: Handmade bust of L. Frank Baum and the characters of his imagination, 1970s.

64: Jigsaw puzzle from England, 1940.

67: Illustration by Anton Loeb, 1950.

69 (top): Illustrations of the White City from a souvenir book for the 1893 World's Columbian Exposition in Chicago, published in 1893.

70–71: Detail from a Mardi Gras poster published as a newspaper supplement, 1908.

77: Woggle-Bug lesson card from an educational game, 1905.

82: Original photograph of Fred Stone from the stage production of *The Wizard of Oz*, 1903.

84: Detail of the lobby card from the 1926 silent film production starring Larry Semon as the Scarecrow.

85 (left): Candy card, Barratt Company, U.K., 1940.

86: Classroom poster issued by the United States Department of Education, 1926.

117: Theater flyer from Spain for the MGM movie, 1947.

130–131: Postcard from the 1903 stage production of *The Wizard of Oz* which featured David Montgomery as the Tin Man and Fred Stone as the Scarecrow. The two actors became famous playing these parts. Although Montgomery died young, Stone spent the better part of his career reprising the role. Bolger, who had seen Stone perform many times, often said he modeled his performance, especially the dance sequences, after Fred Stone.

141 (left): The Wizard of Oz wall hanging by Vic Cantone, 1970s.

142–143: Hungarian LP record album cover, 1980.

148: Postcard advertising the Weeki Wackee Mermaids of Florida, 1967.

150 (center): Hand-tinted postcard from the 1903 stage production of *The Wizard of Oz*.

6 5 4 5 6 6 6 6 6

About the Art

158 (left): Souvenir pewter figures from the MGM Grand in Las Vegas, 1990s. Top: Par-T-Masks merchandise from the MGM movie, 1939. Right: Photograph from 1939.

161: *Screen Romances*, August, 1939.

162–163: Handmade, three-dimensional, iron wall hanging, probably one-of-a-kind, 1980s.

172: John R. Neill illustration hand colored by Rhonda J. Caspar.

181: Rule book cover illustration for *The Wonderful Game of Oz*, a board game from Parker Bros., 1922.

212: Woggle-Bug lesson card from an educational game, 1905.

225: Promotional photographs from the Ice Capades, 1961.

231 (top): Photograph from the 1933 Chicago World's Fair, illustrating the Enchanted Island attraction. Bottom: Stangl plate, Kiddie Ware series, 1960s.

232: Handmade metal sculpture by Andrew Kingham, 1990s.

234: Photograph of Fred Stone and David Montgomery from the 1903 stage play of *The Wizard of Oz*.

250–251: Dick Martin, 3-D advertising structure for *The Visitors from Oz*, 1960.

254 (inset): Comic book adaptation of *The Wizard of Oz, Princess Magazine*, September, 1967.

256–257: Souvenir cookie box issued in conjunction with the 1903 stage production.

280: Photograph of Willard Carroll's Oz room in his house in the Hollywood Hills, California, by Richard Glenn.

281 (top): Dust cover by Dick Martin, 1960. Left: Dust cover by Roycroft, 1959.

292: Judy Garland "Dorothy" doll, merchandise from the MGM movie, 1939.

303: Firecracker label from Macao, 1960s.

323: Puzzle from *Little Oz Books with Jigsaw Puzzles*, 1932.

324–325: Detail from a Whitman jigsaw puzzle, 1939.

330–331: Box cover from a British jigsaw puzzle, 1940.

338: Handmade needlepoint, 1970s.

339 (top): Limited edition animation cel, *Tales of The Wizard of Oz*. Background: Game pieces from a British board game based on *Tales of the Wizard of Oz*, 1961.

341: Decca soundtrack album of the MGM movie, 1948.

342–343: Spanish promotional flyer for the MGM movie, 1947.

344–345: Newspaper supplement illustration featuring the Enchanted Island attraction at the Chicago World's Fair Century of Progress, 1933.

346–352 (background): Conceptual watercolor of the Emerald City, MGM art department, 1938.

Acknowledgments

I first met Willard Carroll in 1998. At the time I was working at a publishing company in New York and Willard sent me a proposal for a book about his *Wizard of Oz* collection. To date, that collection includes more than 30,000 items and, thanks in large measure to Ebay, it continues growing almost daily. As a book editor, I am fascinated by people of passion and Willard more than qualifies. Along with our brilliant book designer, Tim Shaner, we published *One Hundred Years of Oz* and *I, Toto: The Autobiography of Terry, the Dog Who Played Toto*. *All Things Oz* is our third collaboration in the Land of Oz and it just gets more and more interesting every time we work together.

I must also thank my dear friend and editor, Annetta Hanna, who has a rare talent for making everything look easy. Without her enthusiasm and support, this project would have melted away long ago.

Thank you Richard Glenn for your fine photographs and cheerful spirit.

Jack Messitt, Chris Measom, Woolsey Ackerman and Lorie Cox were especially helpful in bringing order to our chaos.

I learned a lot about Oz from *The Annotated Wizard of Oz*, by Michael Patrick Hearn, a fantastically researched book that I highly recommend to anyone interested in Oz, and from John Fricke who wrote the text to *100 Years of Oz*, a book that is a treasured resource for me. On behalf of Oz fans everywhere, I'd like to thank Peter Glassman, publisher of Books Of Wonder in New York, for keeping the Oz books in print.

Thanks to Sarah Stewart Zweibach, whose cheese straws got cut from the final edit, and to Rhonda Caspar for her coloring skills.

I also want to thank everyone at Clarkson Potter, especially Maggie Hinders and Marysarah Quinn.

On a final personal note, I would like to add that this book is lovingly dedicated to the memory of my mother, Norma Deutsch Sunshine, and my aunt, Hannah Deutsch Katz, who alternated the roles of Good Witch and Bad Witch throughout my childhood.

—Linda Sunshine, Los Angeles, 2003